IN THE COMPANY OF
M O O S E

SECOND EDITION

Victor Van Ballenberghe

STACKPOLE
BOOKS

Published by
STACKPOLE BOOKS
5067 Ritter Road
Mechanicsburg, PA 17055
www.stackpolebooks.com

Printed in China

First paperback edition

10 9 8 7 6 5 4 3 2

Text and photographs by the author

A version of "Death of a Warrior" was published on June 30, 2002, in the *Anchorage Daily News*.

ISBN-13: 978-0-8117-1291-0 (paperback)
ISBN-10: 0-8117-1291-5 (paperback)

Cataloging-in-Publication Data is on file with the Library of Congress.

MOST PEOPLE HAVE HEROES. They choose professional athletes, entertainers, historical figures, or perhaps someone they knew well as a teacher or mentor. Paul Errington, my hero, was a biologist who studied predation. He died in 1963 before I became a wildlife biologist, so we never met. Nevertheless, his writing influenced me greatly. I learned a lot from his scientific approach of detailed field observations coupled with sound thinking. But Paul Errington contributed more than sound science: He valued wild places and wild things and encouraged their preservation. In his studies of predation, he had the gift of wisdom, a rare commodity among biologists, and as a result, his views are no less important today than when he first published them. I dedicate this book to his memory.

Contents

Acknowledgments   vii

Introduction   ix

Giants of the Northern Forests   1

Experiences Afield   21

The Autumn Rut   39

*They Live If They Can and
Die If They Must*   73

Cow and Calf   87

Death of a Warrior   107

The Right Stuff   123

Acknowledgments

I am grateful to a large number of people who directly or indirectly contributed much to my moose studies. Richard J. Mackie and James M. Peek first gave me the chance to study moose in Minnesota. Jim Peek has been an esteemed colleague for thirty-five years and participated in the Denali research. Dale Miquelle worked for me at Denali and then went on to do his doctoral dissertation research there. He alone unraveled the mysteries of scent marking and appetite suppression. R. Terry Bowyer and John Kie also contributed much at Denali. Jim MacCracken, Vern Schlatter, Alex Connors, and John Bevins helped with fieldwork and data analysis. Many Denali National Park employees helped administer my research for nearly two and a half decades. Joe Van Horn was there the entire time. Several U.S. Forest Service employees ensured that the work continued, including Ted Dyrness, Richard Werner, the late Ken Wright, Charles Philpot, and Mike Novy. Karl Schneider, Alaska Department of Fish and Game, supported my first Alaska moose and wolf research. Tom Stephenson and Jim MacCracken devoted endless hours of difficult fieldwork to the Copper River Delta study. Judith Schnell and Amy D. Lerner at Stackpole Books edited and improved the manuscript. Finally, Linda S. Masterson, my wife, prodded me to write the story of Big Boy, the first step in producing this book. All of these people and many others deserve credit for their contributions, and they have my sincere thanks.

Mount McKinley, the highest point in North America, looms above moose habitat in central Alaska.

Introduction

This is a book about moose in autumn, a time when moose are sleek and handsome, a season when the northern forests shine with color. For much of the year moose lead uneventful lives, but during the fall mating season they perform behaviors not seen at any other time. There are violent fights in autumn as bulls battle for dominance and mating rights. Autumn in moose country brings excitement as summer ends, winter approaches, and the sounds of moose fights echo in the hills. For many years I have lived in moose country during autumn. I want to share with you the beauty of moose as I have seen it and tell you about the things I have experienced in the company of moose.

For thirty-five years my life has been intertwined with the lives of moose, the giant deer that inhabit northern forests. As a wildlife biologist, I researched moose from Minnesota to Alaska, studying everything from what they ate to how they behaved and how they survived in the presence of bears and wolves. In addition, I spent time in moose country in such far-flung places as British Columbia, Newfoundland, Sweden, and Russia. As a biologist, I spent more time in the field close to wild moose than

Cow moose without calves are often solitary in early autumn.

Moose habitat is often wild and remote.

anyone else, observing their every move and trying to understand how they cope with their environment. Much of this work was published in technical journals and books as my professional contribution to science. But now, as I grow older and my scientific career winds down, I am more taken by the beauty of moose, by their strange grace, by their gentle nature, and by their individual personalities, which vary greatly.

Wildlife biology has changed greatly in recent years. Biologists now spend most of their time in offices using computers. Fieldwork today with large mammals is often done with airplanes or other motorized vehicles. The old-fashioned, naturalistic approach of directly observing wild animals at close range is seldom practiced. In my career I have been fortunate to observe and study moose in a few precious places where moose accepted people, where I could approach them closely without disturbing them and watch as they conducted every detail of their lives. The technique of radio-tracking animals with collars bearing small transmitters allowed me to follow individual moose for periods up to fifteen years. Each animal had its own individual frequency, and with a radio receiver I could locate it at will. This allowed me to follow moose during their lifetimes, observing their successes and failures, births and deaths, and documenting their responses to changes in their environment.

This scientific work opened a new window for me, a window into the lives of moose that would have remained closed had I studied moose only from airplanes. This window also allowed me to know moose as individual beings that varied greatly, not only physically, but also in all aspects of their personalities. And I began to appreciate their beauty and grace and their value to me beyond being merely subjects of scientific studies.

Wildlife biologists are trained to focus on populations, rather than individual animals, and to avoid emotional ties to specific animals. To a certain extent, they must do this to maintain objectivity. But some of the most relevant biological work that has touched the hearts of millions of people worldwide has come from observational studies where biologists had close ties to individual animals. Perhaps the best examples of this are the primate studies of Jane Goodall and Dian Fossey. While contributing a great deal to scientific understanding of primates in the wild, their work went much farther: It captured people's attention and alerted them to the plight of primates and other large mammals in an ever-shrinking natural environment.

As a biologist, I strongly support scientific research and think it essential in providing a framework to solve the environmental problems we face today. But research alone is not enough. People must care for wild things and wild places; they must have a personal stake in preventing environmental problems and solving them after they occur. That stake comes both from personal experiences in the wild and from seeing, hearing, and learning about animals from various media sources. Toward that end, I hope that this book will contribute to better understanding of moose, a magnificent wild species. I further hope that it will provide people with an appreciation of the beauty that moose possess and encourage preservation of the wild lands of the North that moose require in order to survive.

A bull moose wanders near a treeline in mountainous habitat during the autumn rutting season.

A bull moose in Baxter State Park, Maine.

Giants of the Northern Forests

What is a moose? Simply put, moose are giant deer that live in the northern forests of Europe, Asia, and North America. Their closest North American relatives are white-tailed deer, mule deer, elk, and caribou. The deer family includes dozens of other species distributed around the world. All moose, no matter where they live, belong to the same species, but there are several different subspecies that differ in size, color, antler structure, and many other attributes. North American moose include four different subspecies: the large Alaska-Yukon moose, the small Shira's moose of the Rocky Mountains, and two other varieties that range in Canada and the northern United States from the Pacific Ocean to Newfoundland. States with significant moose populations include Montana, Idaho, Wyoming, Colorado, and Utah in the West; Minnesota and Michigan in the Midwest; and Maine, New Hampshire, and Vermont in the East. A few other states, including North Dakota and New York, have small numbers. Moose are not well adapted to heat, and their southern distribution is limited mainly by climate. In places like Utah, they occupy habitats at high elevations where summer temperatures remain relatively low.

About one million moose currently live in North America. Numbers have been relatively stable in recent years in most areas. Moose have expanded their range in the northeastern United States in recent decades, moving westward from Maine into New Hampshire, Vermont, and New York, with stragglers moving into such unlikely places as the outskirts of Boston. Other states, such as Colorado and Michigan, established moose populations through transplants from adjacent areas.

Adult moose are very big. They begin life as twenty-five- to thirty-five-pound newborns. When fully grown, the largest males may exceed sixteen hundred pounds,

Rocky Mountain elk are also members of the deer family.

while big females weigh more than twelve hundred pounds. They are heaviest in autumn after regaining weight lost during winter, at times 35 percent or more of their fall mass. Moose stand up to seven feet tall at the shoulder. The antlers of the largest bulls can span more than eighty inches and weigh seventy-five pounds. Bulls are fully grown by eight years of age; cows by four. Only bulls have antlers. They grow and shed a new set each year.

Moose have long legs, a square-shaped body, a long nose, and a prominent shoulder hump. Long legs allow easier travel through deep snow and better access to aquatic plants in deep water. Square bodies conserve heat in climates where midwinter low temperatures reach sixty degrees below zero. Long noses enhance aquatic feeding and extend the reach of moose to feed on tall shrubs. Bones in the shoulder hump enhance leverage for tendons and muscles that support a very heavy head and antlers.

Moose are giant members of the deer family that inhabit the northern forests of Europe, Asia, and North America.

The front foot, or hoof, of an adult cow moose.

Calf moose have a reddish brown coat that is not spotted, unlike deer fawns or elk calves. By early autumn calves grow the brown-colored hair that adults possess. Adult color varies from nearly black to light brown on the back and sides, with light brown hair underneath and on the lower legs. Dark coats absorb heat from winter sunshine but are a liability in summer and may cause overheating. A few records exist of white or partially white moose, but such animals are extraordinarily rare. By autumn moose have grown a new, thick coat of long hair capable of insulating their bodies from bone-chilling cold that lasts for months in the Far North.

A prominent dewlap, or bell, hangs from the chin of the bull. Cows have much smaller bells or may lack this structure altogether. In young bulls the bell has a dangling tail up to two feet long in addition to a large, fleshy base. Older bulls often lack this tail, having lost it to freezing during the coldest winter weather. The bell of moose is similar to the beard of goats and to other structures found in related species including bison. These are thought to function as display organs that enhance the profile of the head and neck.

All deer possess strong, durable teeth well designed to chew woody plant tissues. They have incisors only on the bottom. These incisors contact a tough upper pad that the lower teeth bear against to snip off twigs and leaves. The rear teeth are sharp and pointed in young animals, gradually wearing down to flat stubs in old age. Very old moose may wear out their dentition, leading to poor nutrition and death. The roots of teeth contain annual growth rings that biologists often use to estimate an animal's age.

The largest antlers of any living deer are grown by bull moose. Unlike many deer species, which have points branching from a single main beam,

Moose leave large, distinctive tracks like this one in soft soil at the edge of a stream.

The largest bull moose weigh up to sixteen hundred pounds.

Moose can browse on plants from ground level to ten feet high.

moose antlers are palmate. This means that rather than a beam, the main part of the antler is a thin, flat plate of bone. This provides flexibility and perhaps reduces serious breakage when bulls crash together in mating season fights. Antlers grow from late March to mid-August, nourished by nutrients obtained from huge quantities of leaves and twigs eaten during spring and summer. Soft at first, they later harden and when mature are dense, white bone consisting mainly of calcium and phosphorus. During the growth phase antlers are covered with a dark, soft skin with short hair, called antler velvet. When antlers are fully grown and the mating season begins, the blood supply to antlers is cut off, nerves die, and velvet is removed by thrashing antlers against shrubs and trees. Further thrashing stains the pure white antlers a rich brown color. For the rest of the mating season, these dead bone structures function as weapons and shields in combat between males.

Like leaves falling from deciduous trees, moose antlers are shed annually after the mating season. Bone dissolves at the junction of the antler base and the skull, allowing the antler to fall to the ground. Both antlers are seldom shed at once; typically, bulls carry one antler a day or more longer before it too falls. Shedding begins in November. By mid-January most bulls are antlerless, but the smallest bulls may retain antlers until April. Shed antlers bleach white if exposed to the sun and soften with decay over time. Porcupines, hares, and other small mammals gnaw on them to obtain the minerals they contain.

Biologists have documented more than 220 different plant species that moose eat, including trees, shrubs, herbaceous plants, and aquatics. Moose are primarily browsers, with most of their diet consisting of twigs and leaves of woody plants, but in some areas, moose focus on nonwoody plants during summer. Where willow shrubs are abundant, moose favor them above all else. Birch, aspen, and balsam fir are eaten heavily when abundant. Some plants, including spruce, contain chemicals that interfere with digestion. Moose avoid these plants. Just as predators and prey engage in an evolutionary arms race, plants and herbivores evolve together,

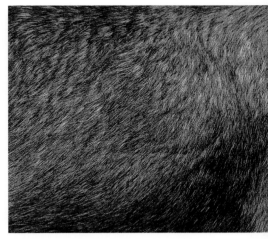

Moose grow dense hair coats that insulate them from intense winter cold.

The rear of this hard antler shows tracks of blood vessels that carried nutrients during the summer growth period.

The skin, or velvet, that covers antlers during growth is shed during autumn and may hang from tree branches.

Antlers are shed annually as bone at the junction of the skull and antler dissolves.

the plants trying to deter browsing, the herbivores trying to become more efficient feeders. Along with chemical defenses, plants evolved thorns and other structures to make it more difficult for plant-eating animals to consume them.

During winter moose break down saplings in order to reach the uppermost twigs. They either pull down high branches with their mouths until the stems break or straddle the plants and walk over them. They may also strip bark off small tree trunks and scrape patches of bark off with their incisors. When snow is deep and moose are concentrated, extreme damage to trees and shrubs occurs, and many plants die.

Deer are ruminants that feed quickly, chew little, and swallow large plant parts for later processing. While resting, they chew their cuds, breaking down the larger particles for more efficient digestion. Their digestive system includes the rumen, a large vat of plant material, liquids, and microorganisms that break down plant tissue into compounds that are absorbed and provide energy. In winter, when forage is fibrous, difficult to digest, and low in nutrients, plant tissue is slow to pass. Moose pellets are the end result, measuring about an inch long and consisting of little more than sawdust. The softer, more digestible diet of early summer results in "moose pies," always a hazard to hikers during summer in moose country.

During summer moose require many dietary components, including sodium, which is rare in certain areas and not very abundant in plants.

Trunks of aspen trees in moose country are often scarred as moose strip them of bark in late winter.

*Moose commonly feed on aquatic plants
to obtain sodium and other nutrients.*

Leaves and twigs of willow plants are important food sources of moose in many areas.

They seek mineral licks, places where water bearing sodium and other compounds seeps from the ground. Moose drink water and eat soil at licks in an effort to acquire sodium, and may spend several hours a day at a lick for a week or more to replenish sodium reserves lost during winter. They may move long distances to occupy a lick, at times even moving outside their normal summer home range. In some areas moose obtain sodium from road salt, drinking and eating on roadsides during spring and summer.

Sharp seasonal variations are normal in moose country. Summer, the season of feeding, is short, barely three months in the Far North. Moose must acquire most of the fat and protein needed for the rest of the year in summer, when green, highly nutritious forage is abundant. As a result, moose feed for much of the day, more than twelve hours in early summer. When not feeding, they rest or move to new feeding areas. Social interactions with other moose are rare, as the animals focus mainly on acquiring energy.

Winter, the season of survival, is long, with snow covering the ground for up to eight months. Plants are snow covered and dormant, and forage quality is poor. Moose reduce their metabolism and activity during winter. They rest during most of the day, reducing their feeding time to half that during summer. Social interactions with other moose again are rare, as the animals are now focused mainly on conserving energy.

Moose are excellent swimmers and often enter ponds, lakes, and streams to feed or to avoid predators.

Cow moose rear calves during summer. Milk provides much nutrition, but calves begin feeding on vegetation when only a few days old.

Moose struggle to survive in winter when deep snow covers food and makes travel difficult.

Female moose usually give birth for the first time when they are three years old. One, two, or very rarely three calves are born. Reports of cows with more than three calves are instances where calves are orphaned or lost and subsequently adopted by a cow already raising calves. Survival of triplets is poor, but twins may survive well in certain populations when predators are scarce and food is abundant. Calf survival is highly variable and ranges from 10 to 80 percent. Calves begin to feed on plants when only a few days old, but most of their nutrition comes from milk for the first six weeks of life.

Weaning occurs by five months of age. Calves stay with their mothers for one year before being driven off just before a new calf arrives. At times yearlings are stubborn and refuse to leave,

Twin calves are commonly born when cows are well nourished.

Early autumn signals the beginning of the mating season for moose.

Moose are well adapted to snow but may starve in severe winters.

Beavers build ponds and create moose habitat.

thereby provoking repeated attacks by the cow. Cows can produce calves each year when in their prime, generally from three to twelve years of age. An older cow may skip reproduction following years when she raises a calf and may retain the yearling for a few additional months, or she may rebond with a yearling after losing a new calf.

Mating season, or the rut, begins in late August as bulls lose their antler velvet. The rut is governed by changes in day length and is remarkably uniform throughout North America. Bulls and cows that socialized little during summer suddenly join each other and show mutual interest. A month of preliminaries occurs before mating begins in late September. Mating lasts for two weeks. Cows generally mate once, but a bull may mate

Willow ptarmigan inhabit forests and tundra along with moose in the Far North.

Red foxes scavenge moose carcasses but are too small to prey upon calves or adults.

with several cows. In some areas bulls seek out individual cows and remain with them for several days until mating is complete. In the Far North, groups of cows assemble with one dominant bull, which retains mating rights to the group by defeating other challengers. Such groups may number twenty or more cows, and a dominant bull that can retain them for the entire rut might mate with them all. By early October the first round of mating is done, but a second round begins three weeks later as cows that failed to conceive become receptive again. After a gestation of nearly eight months, calves are born between mid-May and early June.

Like all mammals, moose live in discrete areas of land called home ranges. These might change seasonally and may vary greatly in size. Some moose spend most of the year in one or two square miles, while others wander over areas twenty-five times as large. Many factors influence the size of an animal's home range, including age and food supply. How do moose choose their home ranges? Females generally use their mothers' areas, having spent a year with them learning boundaries, where to eat, how to travel, and all the other things unique to that piece of country. Males often disperse and choose areas of their own.

Seasonal migrations are common for moose. Areas used in summer might be buried in snow during winter, forcing moose to move to more hospitable habitats. Often this involves shifts in elevation, with moose moving lower during winter. At times migrations take moose long distances, occasionally exceeding one hundred miles, but typically much less. Migratory routes are often traditional, a fact learned by early human

Common loons reside on lakes and ponds that moose use throughout the North.

Seasonal migrations at times involve movements of moose through high mountain passes.

Red squirrels are common residents of northern forests wherever moose are found.

hunters who relied on moose appearing regularly at certain times of year. Moose migrate as individuals, in contrast to elk and caribou, which move in herds.

Moose populations achieve densities ranging from one moose per ten square miles to ten or more moose per square mile. Densities are determined by a myriad of factors, including food supply, climate, predation, and hunting. When habitat quality is high and food is abundant, adult moose survive well and reproduce at high rates. As a moose population increases, it affects its own habitat by heavy browsing of food plants, eventually lowering the amount of high-quality food as plant growth and survival are affected. In time, moose reproduction is lowered and moose numbers decline. When additional stresses, such as deep snow, occur, a population may crash. Biologists refer to the ability of an area to support a certain number of moose as its carrying capacity. When carrying capacity is exceeded, moose numbers decline, perhaps dramatically, and long-term habitat damage is evident.

A moose's wild neighbors in the northern forests include other large herbivores such as white-tailed deer, mule deer, elk, and caribou, as well as mountain sheep and goats, which at times come down from higher elevations to feed side by side with moose. There are also smaller herbivores like snowshoe hares, porcupines, ptarmigan, ruffed grouse, and spruce grouse. For the most part, these species are good neighbors. Much of the time when in close proximity, they ignore each other. But there are more subtle effects, including competition for food. Hares and ptarmigan are cyclic and become incredibly abundant at times. They are the northern

Lynx feed mainly on snowshoe hares but may also scavenge moose carcasses.

Dall's sheep in Alaska and northwestern Canada occupy mountainous habitats, at times descending to lower elevations where moose are found.

equivalents of locust plagues, consuming much of the vegetation in their paths.

A whole host of northern forest predators and scavengers depend on moose meat, at times exclusively, as an energy source. Bears, wolves, and mountain lions are the main predators. Red foxes, coyotes, wolverines, lynx, fishers, pine martens, ravens, eagles, gray jays, and dozens of microorganisms are scavengers. Moose are the centerpiece of the food web for a very large number of animals in the North, including humans. Without them, the northern forests would be much different places.

Snowshoe hares may compete with moose for food when their populations reach cyclic highs.

Experiences Afield

In September 1967 I began a moose study on the Superior National Forest in northeastern Minnesota. This was a land of white pine, black spruce, and aspen, of countless lakes and ponds, and deep woods inhabited by moose, wolves, black bears, white-tailed deer, beavers, fishers, red foxes, and ruffed grouse. Portions of it had been logged and replanted with jack pine. Logging roads and trails provided access into much of the country. Farther north next to Canada was the Boundary Waters Canoe Area, one of the best-known wilderness areas in the United States. To a young man from the East, it was a whole new environment rich with wildlife and wild country, full of opportunity to provide new experiences. I had just recently seen my first wild moose in Yellowstone National Park and had never before observed wild wolves. Now I had the good fortune to spend time in the field in the presence of these exciting creatures at the beginning of my career as a wildlife biologist.

In the early 1960s biologists developed a new technique to study wild animals, one that would revolutionize the field and open new avenues to learn things never before possible. This was radiotelemetry, in which a collar and transmitter were fastened to an animal, allowing biologists to locate it by following its signal with a portable receiver. Prior to this, studying large, elusive animals that lived in remote areas was difficult. Animals were ear-tagged or fitted with numbered or color-coded collars and resighted, but often data were sparse. Telemetry opened the door to learning vastly more than had ever been possible previously.

My study included fitting radios to moose, one of the first such efforts in North America. But first I had to catch the moose, a difficult task that my colleagues and I had greatly underestimated. I used a dart gun that delivered a dose of immobilizing drug to the moose. After about fifteen minutes, the moose collapsed, allowing about forty minutes to attach the collar and ear tags and obtain body measurements before it regained its footing and ran off. Easier said than done. The moose in this area had not been legally hunted in fifty years. I stress, *legally* hunted. The local residents, living on the edge of the wilderness, occasionally shot moose for winter food, and the moose responded by fleeing at the sight, sound, or smell of people or vehicles. To say they were spooky is an understatement.

For the first year I had exactly one moose on the air, a fact my colleagues fretted about, as one moose does not a study make. Ideally, I needed about twenty collared animals. The harder I tried, the worse it got.

An adult cow moose surveys her realm in autumn.

Moose feeding in ponds seemed like sitting ducks until I tried to get within dart gun range, about thirty yards or less. I tried canoeing rivers and lakes, attempting to ambush moose feeding on aquatic plants. I just knew I could outpaddle a moose, but it never happened. Several times darts hit moose and bounced off without delivering the drug. And there were truly discouraging times when everything worked, but warm temperatures reduced the potency of the drug and nothing happened after the hit.

My luck changed the second winter when it snowed. Man, did it snow! In places there were over four feet of snow in the woods. The main logging roads had snowbanks six feet high on either side after they were plowed. Moose got on the roads and wouldn't get off, moving ahead of the plows or running ahead of vehicles rather than wading through snow that quickly tired them. It was bad for moose but good for moose biologists. Now it was just a matter of pursuing a moose with a truck, firing the dart gun out the window, and backing off until the drug took effect. My fortunes as a biologist changed overnight.

One day I discovered a much more sporting way to collar moose, by following a fresh set of tracks on snowshoes. Within about a half mile under those deep snow conditions, moose would tire. I could literally run them down and dart them as they backed up against cover to face me rather than flee. The tricky part was not approaching too closely thereby provoking a charge. I quickly learned that when retreating from a mad moose, you really don't want to be on snowshoes, especially when they tangle and produce a fall. In a few weeks I had the necessary number of animals collared and the study was off to a good start.

Radio collars revolutionized field studies of moose starting in the 1960s.

In northern Minnesota and many other areas, moose use ponds as feeding sites during spring, summer, and fall.

Later, in Alaska, I graduated to using helicopters to capture moose, instead of trucks and snowshoes. It was the only way to work in vast, road-less areas. In one study I collared more than two hundred moose in three years. This was pretty exciting business, flying close to the ground while pursuing moose through the trees. My life depended on the abilities of several highly skilled pilots, including some trained in Vietnam. Tagging moose must have seemed quite tame to them in contrast to having the pursued fire back. Nevertheless, a small error in judgment or a mechanical glitch could have been fatal.

Most of the helicopter captures were routine: Pursue the moose, fire the dart, back off until the moose collapsed, then land and attach the collar. Of course, there were occasional long treks to reach the moose when the ship could not land nearby, or some tense moments landing in tight spots. Helicopters don't respond well then the tail rotor shears off after striking a tree. Several times moose got themselves into difficulty by collapsing at the wrong time in a bad place. One cow broke through the ice of a pond in about six feet of water. I held its head high while my partner administered

This female moose was the first cap-
tured in northern Minnesota and one
of the first moose in North America
to wear a radio collar. She had lost
hair as a result of a parasite called
the winter tick.

the antidote. We focused on saving the moose and failed to attach a collar.
In a few minutes the moose revived, but it couldn't get footing at the
bottom of the pond or on the icy bank to climb out. We returned to base,
got a long rope, and came back ready to pull her out with the helicopter,
a risky venture. Luckily, she escaped on her own while we were gone.

In Denali National Park, where I had a long-term study, moose were
quite tolerant of people and I could approach on foot to within darting
range. This was infinitely better than using helicopters for several reasons.
It did not stress the animals as a helicopter chase did, and it was inexpen-
sive. I did most of this work alone, despite the occasional need to reposi-
tion an immobilized moose by pushing it around, setting it upright so its
breathing was not affected. Again, most of the time things went smoothly,
but there were a few tense moments. One involved a particularly aggressive bull named Grizzly in honor of his color. At a distance he resembled a
bear. Unlike most mature bulls, Grizzly simply did not tolerate people well
during the mating season. In his presence one had to be constantly aware
that he could charge at any moment if people were too close. In such situations you must run. You really do not want an angry sixteen-hundred-
pound bull moose to make contact with you no matter how minor.

During the years Grizzly was collared, I had to change his collar several times as the batteries expired or there were transmitter failures. Often
this was in autumn when his behavior was bad. The drug I was using had
an all-or-nothing effect; when it wore off, the moose was up in an instant,
ready for action. On two occasions I was closer than I should have been
when he jumped up and charged. Experience on my high school track

When snow is extremely deep, moose pursued by
people on snowshoes stand their ground.

team finally paid off and he never caught me, although it was neck and neck for the first few yards.

On another occasion I darted a cow to change her collar. It was during the mating season, and she was part of a small group of other cows and one large, dominant bull. I waited until the collared cow moved off until firing the dart. Just as she collapsed, a small bull approached and stood over her. I carefully moved toward them on the opposite side of the cow and tried to scare the bull off. He was not about to leave, as he finally had possession of a cow after being thwarted repeatedly by the larger bull. He was really quite nice and not very aggressive toward me but was unwilling to let the cow get away. After a time, when he realized the cow was unresponsive, the bull left and I went about my work. On two other occasions, similar things happened with aggressive bulls that needed more persuasion to depart. Even with these rare interruptions, I was always able to get the moose collared and on its way.

Despite their reputation as angry, volatile beasts during mating season, bull moose for the most part are so focused on the tasks at hand that they pose little danger to people. I spent thousands of hours in the field in close proximity to moose during the rut and seldom found them aggressive. But there were exceptions. The bull called Grizzly once chased me into an alder patch, where the top of my pack frame caught on some branches and nearly prevented me from escaping. Once I provoked a charge by a bull with an injured front foot. I was trying to see why he wasn't using the foot when

This bull, named Grizzly, was aggressive toward people in Denali National Park. He had a very prominent bell, or dewlap.

suddenly he regained full use of it and came at me on the run. I resorted to a strategy used previously—run a few steps and fall down. I still recall vividly the feeling of dread as he passed directly over me. Fortunately, there was no contact. His objective was a pond about fifty yards away, and once in the water he felt safe. He didn't realize that fright alone was enough to make me forevermore stay away from "injured" bulls.

Cows with young calves pose a serious threat to people who purposely or inadvertently approach them. During a study of survival of young calves, it was my job to locate pregnant, radioed cows daily until they gave birth, then monitor them to determine if and when the calves died. One year in late May there was still much snow on the ground when cows were giving birth. While on snowshoes one day, I radio-tracked a cow only to suddenly come upon her with a set of newly born twins. Suddenly she charged, and I stepped aside holding the radio antenna up. She hit it and broke off one element. She quickly returned to the calves but came again as I tried to untangle the snowshoes and move off. Luckily there was no contact, and I left the area uninjured.

Moose have severely injured less fortunate people. In the worst cases, death resulted. In Anchorage, Alaska, a bystander videotaped a cow moose attacking an elderly man who blundered into the cow and her calf. It terrified me to see the intensity, speed, and power of the attack and reminded me never to get into a situation like that if it could be avoided. But mainly, after being in the company of moose for thirty-five years, I am more impressed by their gentle nature rather than their aggression. As with most animals, when threatened they respond, but people can learn how to avoid bad situations, how to read the behavior of moose, and how to react if moose are aggressive.

Brown bears are important predators of moose in certain areas.

I also had experiences in the field with other large, potentially dangerous animals like grizzly bears and wolves. The bears were worrisome, as they have a proven record of aggression. On occasion I put myself in situations that could have been bad but fortunately were not. One spring day I tracked the radio signal of a cow and her two-week-old calves. As I got near the signal's source, a raven suddenly flew up about thirty yards away. Bears kill many young calves, and often ravens clean up the remains. I left the area, as I was unsure what had happened and didn't want to encounter a bear defending its kill.

Ten days later I went back to find that a bear had killed the cow moose and her calves and undoubtedly was there when I approached the first time. Over the course of many years, I tracked cows and their calves hun-

Gray wolves are also important moose predators.

dreds of times but never came this close to provoking a bear attack. Sometimes good luck is more important than anything else in avoiding trouble.

One of my colleagues survived a full-blown grizzly bear charge while doing fieldwork on our moose study. He was radio-tracking some moose far from the road when he saw several moose ahead. He rounded a bend on a moose trail and was suddenly too close to a large bear. Standard advice in bear country is never to run from a bear, but my colleague was so frightened and the bear was so close that he sprinted off, only to trip and fall after a few seconds. The bear pursued him but ran past only a few feet away as he was still on the ground.

My own close encounters with grizzlies included a few bluff charges that were nullified by standing my ground and many other experiences where bears retreated or avoided me. Early on I learned never to travel much in thick-cover bear country without making noise. Most of the time grizzlies were no more interested in trouble than I was and moved off as soon as they heard, smelled, or saw me.

I had many opportunities to see moose respond to bears. At times the moose ran off in panic. At other times they seemed aware but not very concerned. And rarely they were aggressive, including successfully driving off bears that were trying to prey upon young calves. Once during the rut I watched a bear move among a group of about a dozen rutting moose, none of them too concerned with its presence, at times only a few yards away. Another time I saw a female grizzly with two cubs approach a rutting group. A young bull detected them and ran back to the scattered group. On cue, the moose all formed a tightly packed core and stared as the bears moved within one hundred yards and stood up to stare back. For a minute or two neither moose nor bears moved. Then the bears retreated and the moose went back to their rutting activities.

In mid-September in Denali National Park, I encountered a shuttle bus on the park road watching a large bear about three hundred yards away. Passengers had just seen the bear chase, catch, and kill an adult cow moose. Everyone on the bus was quiet, totally in awe of what had just transpired. Other bus passengers in spring witnessed bears catching young moose calves. A bear once killed the calf of a radioed cow in the parking lot of the train depot at Denali. I vividly recall the stealth and skill of a large grizzly that I watched during a ten-day period one spring as it caught four sets of moose twins in one area of the park. Some bears are calf specialists for about six weeks each spring, spending most of their time searching for and pursuing cows with calves.

Although wolves provoke fear in many rural residents of moose country, the chance of being injured by a normal wolf unfed by people, and therefore fearless, is about the same as being struck by lightning. In my fieldwork I encountered wolves often. In Minnesota they were more scared of people than were moose, having been shot and trapped for decades. They were so abundant during my years there that often one or more darted across a logging road in front of the truck, gray ghosts that disappeared at once into the forest. A local resident on the shore of Lake Superior let his small dog out early one morning, only to have it chased back

I studied this pack of wolves with twenty members in Alaska.

onto the porch by a young wolf. The door slammed shut behind the wolf, and there followed a period of confusion as dog, wolf, and man moved quickly around the porch, each trying to escape.

In Alaska I conducted wolf research in addition to my moose studies and had the good fortune to spend about a thousand hours in small airplanes radio-tracking wolves and moose in remote areas. Wolves depend on moose, caribou, mountain sheep, beavers, and other animals in Alaska. At times moose are their main prey. As a result, I got to see wolves hunt moose on many occasions. As in other studies throughout North America, I often saw unsuccessful chases. Wolves are able to kill only about 10 percent of the moose they encounter, as many moose outdistance wolves or stand and defend themselves. No matter how many or how strong, wolves can seldom penetrate the buzz saw defense of an angry moose kicking with all four feet. They quickly learn how difficult it is and soon leave, hoping to find another moose they can catch while running.

Often I arrived on the scene during a chase or just after a kill. On only two occasions did I witness the entire sequence from beginning to end. One involved two wolves and two moose. As the wolves approached, the moose ran downhill and split up. One wolf pursued each moose. After about a half mile, the wolf I was watching was about fifty yards behind its moose but couldn't seem to close the gap. Then it suddenly accelerated and grabbed the moose's rear leg. I expected to see the moose whirl and buck, trying to disengage the wolf, but instead it mainly just stood there, perhaps too exhausted to fight after the chase. The wolf held on for several minutes. The moose then lost its footing, and the wolf grabbed it behind the neck. After a time the moose died. Instances of a single wolf killing a moose are rare.

A second case involved a pack of ten wolves and a cow with her ten-month-old calf. The pack was traveling along a hillside and flushed several moose but pursued none of them. The cow and calf detected the wolves about two hundred yards off and ran. The wolves gave chase, with three or four quickly closing the gap. The calf ran in front of its mother, the two at times only a foot or two apart. Suddenly one wolf dashed around the cow and grabbed the rear leg of the calf. Several wolves milled around, and in the melee the cow lost her footing and two wolves tried to grab her. She was up in a flash and ran off, while the wolves quickly killed the calf and began feeding.

Of all my experiences in the field, I treasure most these two rare episodes of wolves and moose engaged in the eternal struggle of life and death. But I have had many other encounters with wild wolves that I well remember. On numerous occasions I have heard wolves howling, at times because I invaded their territory, at

The Copper River Delta in Alaska contains lush moose habitat that supports a dense moose population.

A cow moose surveys her domain with the Alaska Mountain Range in the background.

other times because they were communicating with each other. No other sound in nature arouses such primal responses in me as the howling of wolves. Perhaps it is because wolves require wild, healthy land in order to survive, or maybe when I hear mournful howling it reminds me of the centuries of warfare that wolves have survived with people whose goal was to eliminate them.

Finally, my experiences with wolves included studying one pack for three years as it grew from seven to twenty. In the third year the pack had two dens and raised two litters, somewhat unusual for wolves. I captured the alpha male of this pack and collared him. He was one of the most magnificent animals I have ever seen—large, beautiful, in peak condition, and in the prime of his life. During the final winter, he led the pack over long distances, at times following trails made earlier in deep snow. When the pack crossed barren areas, it provided a true spectacle of nature, twenty wolves strung out single-file moving over a wild, snow-covered landscape. Because we had located the pack numerous times, they were totally unafraid of airplanes and at times would sleep as we circled overhead. Later that winter hunters using airplanes shot eighteen of the twenty wolves, including the alpha male. I have always deeply mourned the fact that my research project made the wolves unafraid and cost them their lives.

To me, moose country contains some special places. Some I visited often and knew intimately. Others were seldom seen, and one special place captured my attention only once. But regardless of my time spent there, each place had not only moose, but also moose habitat—special trees, beautiful mountains, pure rivers and lakes, and wonderfully colored leaves in autumn. In these places there were also opportunities to experience waterfowl migrating overhead, to see voles scampering over the forest floor, to watch male grouse displaying to females, or to witness red squirrels busily cutting spruce cones for winter. These were ordinary enough events elsewhere but were special to me because of the nearby presence of moose and the unique nature of the locations.

Of the scores of watercourses in the Minnesota moose study area, one river was special. To get there I had to drive a rough, old logging road long since abandoned by loggers. Then the canoe had to be dragged down a hill to the river's edge. I went there mainly because the river was wide and shallow and the aquatic plants that moose love grew there in abundance. In this half-mile-long pool as many as six to eight moose might feed at once in the early evening hours. A stealthy biologist in a camouflage-colored canoe with some brush in the bow might just be able to dart an unsuspecting moose near shore and collar it there. At least I thought so, but it never happened. Mainly, I suffered black fly bites and tired shoulders from all that paddling. But the river was special, with its quiet current, tall trees nearby, loons, beavers, and fish. After three or four trips there with no success at capturing moose, I could have crossed this river off my list. After all, there were lots of moose in many other places. But I continued to spend evenings there, as much to enjoy the quiet isolation as to look for moose. Perhaps moose also thought the river was special. Maybe I shouldn't disturb them.

In Alaska I studied moose in several places, including the Copper River Delta. This was in the Prince William Sound area, which included a vast landscape of coastal moose habitat uplifted during the 1964 earthquake. Moose there lived a much different life than elsewhere in Alaska, as the maritime climate most of the time freed them of the deep snow and biting cold found farther inland. The delta and its surrounding uplands were some of the most productive moose habitat in Alaska, and moose thrived there.

One late winter day we were collaring moose by helicopter on the east delta, the most remote part of the area. It was warm, clear, and calm weather that some years seems to occur on only a very few days in this land of wind and rain. The late winter sun was

melting snow and spring was not far away. The helicopter had to return to our base, fifty miles west, so I stayed alone at the edge of a small lake for a couple of hours while the ship and the rest of the crew departed. I was a very long way from the nearest human being or human structure. There were no signs that anyone had ever been at this location. It was utterly silent except for the sounds of a few small birds feeding nearby. No airplanes flew overhead. I thought that it was probably the only time in my life I had been this completely removed from civilization. When I heard the distant sound of the helicopter returning, I was sorry the time had passed so quickly. Although I continued the moose work on the delta several more years, I never returned to the small, quiet lake. A second visit there might have been one too many.

A yearling moose browses at the edge of a pond after a spring snowstorm.

Traditional rutting areas attract bulls and cows each year during the mating season.

In Denali National Park there were several special places. One was at the head of a small drainage. It was a ten-acre patch of old spruce trees that moose used nearly every year as a traditional rutting area. The trees were tucked against the foothills of the Alaska Range. Behind the trees were dense alder thickets; above them were rocks and snow during early October, the peak of the rut. I don't know the age of the trees, but they were as big as spruce trees get in the uplands. I collected some six- to eight-foot-tall spruce in this area once and cut the two-inch-thick trunks to determine their ages. Some were forty-five years old, so I imagine the biggest trees were ancient. In places under the widely spaced trees were dense growths of grass, at times reaching four feet in height.

Several of my collared moose spent the rut there, including Grizzly, the aggressive male, during the years that he was the dominant bull in the area. It was a long hike to reach the area, but for several years I went often. It was not a place where people normally hiked. I saw others passing by there only two or three times. It was a good place to gather data on rutting behavior, but I also enjoyed the wonderful view of the Alaska Range to the southeast, and seeing moose moving gracefully among the trees and grass much as they had each autumn for centuries.

A second traditional rutting area was also a patch of spruce but much larger. It wrapped around the base of a hillside and stretched for more than a half mile east to west. It bordered one of the major rivers in the area, near the mouth of a wonderful, big valley. The headwaters extended several miles into the high country of the Alaska Mountain Range. For years this was the place to be in September and October to observe rutting moose. They were there in abundance. Often the main group was twenty or more strong. One day I estimated a total of forty animals in about half the area, truly an unusually high number. At the peak of the rut, about October first, forty moose create a spectacle worth seeing as they run about with bulls chasing cows and each other, branches breaking, and moose calling loudly.

Unlike several of the other special places, I shared this one with many other people. There were research colleagues who daily hiked there and back to spend time recording data. There were visiting wildlife biologists, some of whom had not previously seen rutting moose. I spent a lot of time there with photographers. Some came to film moose as part of television productions aired worldwide. Others were still photographers eager to get images not possible elsewhere. Several writers hiked with us, as did wildlife artists gathering reference material for their paintings.

To get there we had to hike through nearly two miles of dense shrubs growing on spongy tundra. It wasn't an easy stroll. Halfway there we crossed a stream that froze in autumn from the bottom up, thereby raising the water level. This required boots taller than our hiking boots, creating the problem of either bringing extra boots or getting wet feet. For a time I carried a few paper towels each day to dry bare feet after removing my boots and plunging in. Done quickly, it's not all that bad. And there were quite a few days when I carried others across, preferably small, light women, but once or twice men who weighed as much as I did.

A famous photographer solved the stream-crossing dilemma by leaving a pair of hip boots stuck in

Bearberry leaves turn bright red during autumn in tundra areas.

Moose occupy open tundra areas during autumn in the western part of Denali National Park.

willow stems a few feet off the ground on the bank. I warned him that a bear would find them, but he ignored the advice. One morning the boots were gone, carried off by a bear about a hundred yards upstream, but otherwise unharmed. Perhaps the bear was more than just curious, using the boots himself to avoid wet feet.

On a very cold and snowy October morning one year, my assistant and I hiked to a portion of this area for a day of moose watching. I called this place the triangle. It was an alluvial fan shaped like a triangle, a large amount of gravel and soil deposited centuries ago by a swift stream at the base of a mountain. The soil was productive and supported a dense growth of willows, creating perfect habitat for moose during the rut with the spruce forest nearby. On this day we witnessed nonstop action as twenty-two cows and twelve bulls interacted at the peak of the rut. Several cows were ready to mate that day, and the dominant male was frantic trying to keep the other bulls at bay so he could mate with each cow in turn. The task was too difficult, and some of the subdominant males succeeded in driving cows to the edge of the group and fighting among themselves. Cows that were not receptive were constantly harassed by the younger bulls, protesting all the while with the loud, wavering moans that moose cows utter. Of all the days I spent in the company of moose in autumn, this one stands out as very special because of the magnitude of the action. In the years since, as the moose population declined, groups this large no longer formed. I will probably never again experience the drama acted out that day at the triangle, when moose were everywhere and there were no breaks in the action.

At the western end of the Denali Park road, there are moose living on the tundra in September. In most other places they are found in trees or tall shrubs. On the tundra they are more visible, with their large bodies and long legs evident in the low vegetation. The dense alder patches nearby provide cover into which moose disappear, but they soon reemerge into the open areas. Numerous ponds in the area provide feeding sites, and moose use them until late in the season. But this area is special mainly because the moose live in the shadow of Mount McKinley, the tallest peak in North America. From the north side it is awe inspiring, rising up from the lowlands, snow covered yearlong for two-thirds of its height. In September on clear, blue-sky days, when the tundra is red and Mount McKinley forms the backdrop, this moose country has no equal.

Because the moose are so easily accessible, and because of the spectacular setting, photographers from around the world go there after competing for Park Service photography permits. Some of the world's best wildlife photographers have taken moose pictures there. I shared their joy in this special place. But I often wondered if their total concentration on photography denied them the chance to absorb all the wonderful benefits of being there. Of course they wanted to work while the good weather held, as their permits might extend for only a few days. And they had a lot of money invested in the trip. But when I was photographing there, I often put my camera down and simply enjoyed the moment. The human eye can capture things no camera can, and the experiences that result are worth more, in the end, than any photograph.

Sparring is practice fighting that results in no winners or losers or serious injuries.

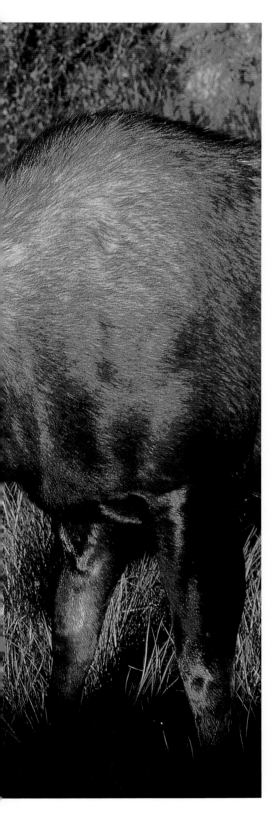

The Autumn Rut

I first learned how strongly the behavior of moose in autumn contrasts with that during the rest of the year by trying to estimate how much food a wild moose eats per day. This seemingly unimportant detail actually is critical to understanding a great deal of the biology of moose. As with all animals, the energy intake and expenditure of moose determine their survival. Biologists interested in how a moose population responds to its habitat must know the amount of food available, how the food supply is used by moose, and at what rate. They need to understand the energetics of moose, and a great deal of research has been devoted to this subject, both by studying captive moose and by observing moose in the wild. An important and basic first step is to determine how much food a moose consumes each day, see how this varies over time and space, and obtain good estimates for both cows and bulls, as bulls are much larger and can be expected to eat more.

In the Denali National Park moose study, we had the ideal opportunity to determine daily food intake, as wild moose there allowed us to observe them at close range as they fed. I should say that most of the moose tolerated our close presence. Some did not, so we chose the most tolerant animals to observe, including some we had radioed. Over time they learned we were harmless.

This was a unique study. Other researchers had used tame moose, taking them out to feed in a variety of habitats, and there were some efforts to observe wild moose feeding in other places, but none generated good data. As moose fed on the leaves and twigs of shrubs during summer, we were able to count bites, determine bite rates, and estimate bite sizes for several of the most important plant species in the moose diet. This was no easy task. At times moose were in dense cover and it was hard to see exactly how they fed. At other times moose

Resting and feeding are the main activities of moose during summer. Social behavior is very rare.

were frightened, perhaps by predators nearby, and didn't cooperate. Even during the best of times, keeping all those bites separate and identifying species was hard. But we were able to devote enough time over the course of four summers to gather good data on bite rates and bite sizes, and by combining these we knew something about food intake rates.

Next we needed to know how much time moose spent feeding each day. We had to determine the activity budget of moose. Daily feeding time combined with bite rates and bite sizes would produce estimates of daily food consumption. The best way to know about activity budgets is to watch individual moose for twenty-four-hour periods, recording their activity periodically. Again, this was difficult. We needed cooperative moose and several crews of patient people, able to stay awake at night, be alert for grizzly bears, and fend off hordes of hungry mosquitoes in mid-summer. My job was to coordinate the entire operation, changing crews every six hours, walking long distances at all times of the day and night as the moose and their human spies moved around the landscape.

And so I learned that in summer, moose feed a lot. They are driven to process as much food and obtain as much energy as they can before winter starts to drain their energy reserves. I also learned that most of the time moose lead very uneventful lives and do little else besides feed, move, and rest. Our summer activity budgets indicated that moose spent less than 3

During summer moose feed as long as thirteen hours per day and process enormous quantities of leaves and twigs.

percent of their time, only about a half hour per day, doing things unrelated to finding food, eating, and resting. Very rarely did they interact with other moose or respond to other species, including predators. We replicated this work in winter and found much the same result. Moose spent much more time resting than in summer, but feeding, resting, and moving constituted all but a tiny fraction of their daily winter activities.

For moose, everything changes in autumn. Uneventful lives are suddenly transformed into days of less feeding and resting, many more interactions with other moose, and behaviors not seen at any other time. As summer turns to autumn in moose country and the first frosts begin to color the foliage, moose transform themselves into different creatures. Winter survival and summer feeding give way to autumn mating season, a time when everything is less important than reproduction. For me, it was by far the most exciting time to be in the field, spending time with moose, watching the rutting season unfold.

Actually, the transformation from summer feeding to autumn rutting takes place gradually, beginning well before the first frosts arrive. By early August bulls have gained a lot of weight, and their antlers are nearly fully grown. Cows, too, are sleek and fat. Those without calves may form small groups for a day or two, jointly using patches of good habitat while feeding and resting together. Bulls often form short-term bonds with each other in late summer, at times staying with one or two companions for a few days before moving off and perhaps joining with different animals. But these associations are brief and mainly based on common use of habitat. Moose at this stage rarely interact much, and bulls and cows are just beginning to show a little interest in each other.

In late August the rutting season begins when the velvet is shed from the antlers of bulls. Bulls that during summer are very protective of their growing antlers suddenly begin to thrash them violently against shrubs and trees, trying to remove the outer skin to expose their fully developed organs of combat made of dead bone. Mature bulls begin this first, with smaller bulls delaying two weeks or more. This is an active process, with bulls vigorously trying to be velvet-free quickly. Strips of velvet hang down, at times visibly annoying the bulls. They may even chew on the velvet they can reach in an effort to be rid of it. Some bulls shed their velvet before its blood supply is fully cut off. Their antlers are stained red in contrast to the bone white color of others. As bulls continue to thrash shrubs, their antlers are stained a deep brown on the outer surfaces, while the inner palms of the larger bulls

remain light colored. I have seen flashes of these in the sun at distances of two miles when the rest of the moose's body was invisible.

Our studies of rutting behavior began with descriptions of the behaviors that moose displayed. At Denali National Park we were able to do more than other biologists had done because moose were abundant and observable in most habitats. We could approach them closely without disturbing them or putting ourselves in danger. We had a unique opportunity to be with moose as they did everything that full-time, professional wild moose do. It was not always easy, as we often had long hikes in rough country, and at times the weather was cold and snowy. But for me it was a wonderful professional opportunity, and I tried to make the most of it for more than twenty years.

An adult bull moose feeds in early autumn.

After five years and about a thousand hours of watching moose in autumn, patiently recording exactly what they did, we had a good catalog of rutting behavior. We also recorded the frequency and duration of each behavior and developed autumn activity budgets so we could estimate how much time moose devoted to each behavior. We separated cows from bulls, as their behaviors were greatly different, and we classified bulls as small, medium, and large, as the mature, largest males did most of the mating. We divided the rutting season into early, middle, and peak periods to see how behaviors changed in occurrence as autumn progressed. Mating took place only during the peak of the rut in late September and early October. We also examined behavior of bulls in different social situations, including when they were alone, when they were with other bulls, and when they were in mixed groups of bulls and cows.

At Denali most moose spend the rutting season in groups. These form in early September as cows without calves aggregate. Unstable at first as individual animals come and go, the groups become more stable by mid-September. On average they include six to seven moose, but those exceeding a dozen are common, and we saw as many as thirty-six in a single group. Moose are not very social, and they generally don't like each other very much, so tensions run high when they aggregate. Cows often react with aggression when others come too close. Each group has a dominant bull, a large, mature male that defends the cows from other bulls. Although bulls chase or herd cows, trying to control their presence in the group, bull moose do not hold harems like certain other species such as elk, which gather females and keep them from leaving. Some female moose do not join groups or join for only brief periods when they mate. Cows with

Shedding of antler velvet in early autumn signals the beginning of the rut or mating season.

calves avoid other moose during all seasons to reduce predation on calves—groups are much easier for predators to find than single moose because groups are more visible and leave more odors—but some cows brave the danger and bring their calves to groups, where the bulls are, for brief periods at the peak of the rut. Most of our observing was done with moose groups, as that is where most of the animals were located. Ninety-six percent of all the moose we observed during autumn were with one or more other moose.

Mating Behaviors

Like other large mammals, moose display a wide array of behaviors, and they share certain ones in common with their close relatives, the other members of the deer family. During the rutting season, males court females, mate with them, and compete with other males, at times in violent fights. Males spar with each other, a form of practice fighting. Females avoid males until it's time to mate; they interact with other females, at times aggressively. There are threats and displays, submissive behaviors, and various other social behaviors that are part of the contacts among individuals that happen during the rut. Each species has its own specific behaviors in addition to those shared with family relatives, and moose differ greatly from white-tailed deer, mule deer, elk, and caribou in several important behavioral acts.

The vocal sounds that moose emit are unique. For much of the year, bulls are quite silent, but as the rut begins with velvet shedding in late August, bulls advertise their presence with a strange, low-frequency vocalization that sounds like a gulp. We termed it a croak. As they move across the hills and through the spruce forests, bulls utter this sound several times per minute, varying its volume. At times, on still autumn evenings, I've heard bulls a half mile away. Other bulls often approach this sound, hoping to see their potential rival. Several variations of this croak are given in

Remaining blood left from velvet shedding stains moose antlers for a day or two before they begin to take on a rich brown color.

At the start of the rut bulls and cows form temporary groups that may persist only a short time.

different social contexts, including a loud version bulls use to herd cows and a much softer courtship sound. Cows utter a long, wailing moan when pestered by bulls. They have no mating call to attract partners, but rather their moaning is a protest. Each cow has her own individual voice; some are low pitched while others are high. Some moans are very long and loud while others are barely audible. The loudest can be heard over a mile away by people and much farther by moose. Both bulls and cows also emit roars when frightened or otherwise highly agitated. Frustrated young bulls kept from cows by large males may run at cows while roaring, in hopes of frightening them from groups and away from large males.

Once antler velvet is shed, bulls spend a lot of time thrashing shrubs and small trees with their antlers in another attempt to advertise their presence or to threaten other moose. Unlike white-tailed deer, moose do not rub trees early in the rut to establish visual marks or signposts. They do this after the main rutting period is over in mid-October and as late as early December. Bush thrashing is distinct from rubbing and signposting behavior, as thrashing is auditory rather than visual. The rate of bush thrashing by bulls is high throughout the rut, several times per hour for large males. Rival bulls about to fight thrash loudly and often. Bulls wandering in search of cows thrash and croak, and they investigate these sounds when other bulls make them.

In early September large bulls stop feeding and eat nothing for about two weeks. They resume feeding gradually during the peak of the rut. Smaller bulls and cows feed during the entire rutting period. As they cease feeding, bulls begin to scent mark. Their urine changes greatly and acquires a strong, pungent odor. Complex chemical compounds called pheromones appear in their urine. Bulls paw shallow pits with their forefeet, digging away ground litter and live plants until they expose soil in pits measuring about a foot wide and eighteen inches long. They urinate in the pits, and then splash the mud and urine onto their heads, antlers, and necks. They then lie down, thereby labeling the undersides of their bodies with the urinary compounds. Large bulls dig up to four or five pits each day during the rut and by late September are so smelly that people can detect them at great distances.

Cows are strongly attracted to the urine of bulls at this time and often run to a bull as he urinates. They sometimes try to force bulls out of pits so they can wallow. They also splash and wallow in the mud and urine, trying to label their bodies. In large groups several cows compete for the pits, often chasing each other and occasionally striking rivals with their forefeet. Normally placid cows are frenzied as they eagerly respond to the scent of bulls.

Bull moose court cows with a mixture of behavioral acts that involve sounds, approaches, body postures, and body contact. They flick their tongues and lick their lips as they approach females in slow motion, hold-

During the rut bulls spend much time thrashing their antlers against shrubs and trees in order to advertise their presence to other moose.

ing their heads low with antlers tilted back. They croak softly. Cows are afraid of bulls, as bulls herd and chase them on occasion to try to control them. If bulls are too aggressive when courting, cows simply retreat. Bulls test the readiness of cows to mate by smell. A bull samples the cow's urine, holding his head high, extending his muzzle, and curling his lips. The German term for this action is *flehmen*. A small gland on the upper palate can sample odors and determine the status of a cow's reproductive cycle. If she is receptive, the bull follows her, trying to rest his chin on her rump. Females may court males by smelling them or rubbing against them. Mounting and mating follow. In northern areas where males control female groups, cows nearly always mate only once per year.

Of all the various mating season behaviors, fighting among bulls is the most dramatic. Fighting settles battles for dominance. It may occur at any time after antlers are velvet-free but is most common during the peak of the rut when cows are ready to mate. Fights have a beginning, middle, and end. They begin as two males approach each other with a slow, deliberate walk, each bull tilting its head and antlers from side to side. When they are nose-to-nose, each displays his body and antlers to the other, slowly twisting his head with eyes open wide and ears lowered. These threats, along with pawing the ground and bush thrashing, can last many minutes. Often one bull is intimidated and quickly runs off. If both persist, the middle part of the fight consists of one to many clashes in which antlers slam into each other and each bull tries to push the other back. One bull may suddenly disengage and whirl around in a complete circle, only to clash again. Those who have seen clashes are forever impressed by the power, strength,

Bush thrashing often results in branches adhering
to antlers until bulls can work them free.

Young bulls may smell larger bulls that have wallowed in rutting pits and labeled their antlers and bodies with chemicals found in the urine of mature bulls.

speed, and determination of bull moose, which may at other times appear slow and ungainly. After a series of clashes that lasts from a few minutes to several hours, the fight ends as one bull suddenly turns and runs off. The winner may pursue the loser and try to gore him, or may escort his rival out of the area.

In contrast, sparring matches are practice fights. Two or more bulls may be side by side when suddenly they engage their antlers and begin gently pushing each other. It resembles a wrestling match where the opponents are more interested in a workout than in striving to win. There are few threats and no real violence. Sparring is often interrupted by other activities, only to resume again and again by the same partners or with different bulls. It is one of the most common behaviors of bulls during and after the main rutting season.

Our rutting season moose activity budgets showed that despite all the intense social behavior, bulls and cows both had time for other things. Cows spent nearly three-quarters of their time feeding and only 2 percent reacting to males. Dominant bulls spent about 40 percent of their time standing as they monitored the cows in their group, resting as the females fed. Bulls spent 14 percent of their time interacting with other moose of both sexes.

My colleagues and I were interested in more than just describing moose behavior; that was merely the first step. Much more interesting was the next phase, developing and testing hypotheses that explained the function of these behaviors. Moose evolved certain behaviors for definite reasons, and they invested a lot of energy and time performing them. As we observed moose during the rutting season, we posed numerous questions. Why did moose label themselves with the urine of bulls? Why did large bulls cease feeding for two weeks? Which bulls were most successful in mating with cows, and what factors determined their success? What was the function of the bell, that loose flap of skin under the chin? Why did young males spend so much time sparring? Why did mature bulls risk death by fighting? After we catalogued rutting behavior, we set about conducting studies to answer these and other questions.

Scent Marking

Moose are not the only mammals to mark themselves with male urine. Actually, it is done commonly by a wide variety of species. Some urinate directly on portions of their body; others deposit urine on the ground and transfer it to the body as moose do. Biologists studying house mice demonstrated that female mice seek male urine, and found that chemicals in the urine prime females for mating by inducing ovulation. Could the main function of scent marking in moose be similar, thereby making moose larger versions of mice? Or were there other functions of this behavior distinct from mice or even distinct from species much more closely related to moose?

We knew from our earliest observations that shortly after large bulls stopped feeding, their urine had a strong, pungent odor that even we could smell at great distances. We also knew that rutting pits were visually obvious. Because bulls dug several pits per day, and because pits were not reused, the area occupied by a bull soon contained a large number of obvious pits. Male or female moose entering this area would quickly see such

Cows may rub their heads together as a form of greeting during the rut.

pits even if they had no odor. Pits might therefore function to transmit information visually, through odor, or by a combination of the two. But was such information directed at cows or at other bulls?

Many other biologists had previously studied scent marking, and there were several published hypotheses to explain its purpose. One proposed that odors from scent marking provide males with a symbol of their dominance. High-ranking males might conserve energy and minimize fighting risks by advertising their rank to other males. Another suggested that odors advertise status to other males. A mature male ready to fight may advertise this status by signaling his physical condition through certain chemicals in urine. A third idea was that strong urine odors might mask from other males a decline in physical condition or status. Masking might enable a bull to extend his rutting activity. Finally, the mouse hypothesis suggested that scent marking is directed at females, not males, with chemicals in male urine affecting the timing of mating.

Each hypothesis had several predictions that could be tested with field observations. If odors advertise male body condition or status, pit digging should occur commonly by all bulls early in autumn, as all are in good condition then. Late in the rut, as large males decline in condition, they should reduce or stop scent marking. Smaller bulls that are excluded from rutting by large bulls, and whose condition is therefore better, should scent mark more during the peak of the rut. Large bulls in poor condition might cheat late in the rut by using pits dug by smaller bulls in better condition.

During the rut moose label their bodies with chemicals found in the urine of mature bulls. Bulls first dig a shallow pit into the soil.

Bulls urinate into rutting pits after digging them with their forefeet.

Bulls splash the mud and urine mixture onto their antlers and heads by stomping the rutting pit with their forefeet.

Bulls and cows wallow in rutting pits to mark themselves with chemicals that are important to the timing of mating by females.

If odors advertise fighting ability, only larger bulls should dig pits, as smaller bulls don't fight larger ones and need not advertise. Pits should be dug to coincide with the peak of the rut, when fights are most common, if scent marking is related to fighting.

If scent marking functions to mask poor condition of large males, it should occur at constant levels during early, middle, and peak periods of the rut. Large bulls trying to cheat by wallowing in pits of other bulls should use the pits of smaller bulls, because they are in better condition later in the rut.

Is scent marking directed at males to provide visual information? If so, then pit digging should be performed more often in the presence of males than females, and males should spend little time smelling pits if they are mainly visual signals. Do bulls visit pits more often than cows? If pits mainly convey information to bulls, be it visually or through odors, cows should be much less interested in pits than bulls.

The mouse hypothesis predicts that scent marking should occur before mating so that females have time to be primed, that large bulls should scent mark early in autumn, and that small bulls should rarely dig pits, as they are excluded from mating by large bulls. Bulls that do not scent mark should cheat by using the pits of other bulls. Furthermore, cows should show intense interest in pits, should apply the urine of bulls to their bodies by wallowing in pits or rubbing against bulls, and should compete with other cows for the use of pits.

Field observations indicated that yearling males did not dig pits, and that small bulls estimated to be two or three years old dug pits rarely. Most scent marking was by larger, older bulls. The urine of small bulls had little odor in contrast to the strong, pungent smell produced by large bulls. Pit digging was most common in the middle stages of the rut and peaked prior to mating. Small bulls responded more to the pits of other bulls than did large bulls. Bulls wallowing in the pits of others were nearly always small bulls. Large bulls aggressively tried to prevent other bulls from using their pits.

Cows never dug pits. They did show intense interest in pits, splashing and wallowing vigorously, and at times trying to displace bulls. Cows competed for pits by threatening and occasionally striking other cows, and by attempting to displace each other from wallows. All of this attention to pits quickly waned as urine in pits was used up by moose or lost its freshness. Cows seldom rubbed the bodies of small bulls but often contacted

Cows compete vigorously for the opportunity to wallow in rutting pits.

large bulls, apparently attempting to acquire urine from them in addition to that obtained in pits.

What did we conclude from all this? The field observations clearly indicated that the function of scent marking in moose was not related to visual characteristics of rutting pits, but rather was based on the compounds found in the urine of bulls. It was also clear that scent marking by bulls was directed at cows rather than at other bulls. Scent marking appeared unrelated to advertising the dominance, rank, status, or condition of bulls, or to the masking of poor condition. Indeed, with regard to scent marking, it appeared that moose resembled large mice, and the behavior served to prime females for mating.

Cows that were strongly attracted to the urine of bulls provided bulls the chance to court them. Females might otherwise avoid males until ready to mate. Small bulls, unable to produce attractive urine, capitalized on this by wallowing in pits of large bulls, acquiring attractive odors, and thus the attention of cows. Such cheating had little risk, but large bulls tried to prevent it by keeping cheaters out of their pits.

Mature bull moose devote much of their time to rutting behavior during the mating season and cease feeding for about two weeks.

During the peak of the rut in late September, bulls resume feeding.

Why should bulls try to induce mating in cows and affect the timing of conception? A critical factor in the survival of calves is the timing of their birth. If born too early, calves may die, as females lack the green forage necessary to produce high-quality milk. If born too late, calves may fail to grow large enough to survive harsh winters. And birth dates are largely determined by conception dates. Survival of calves determines the reproductive success of their parents, and thus bulls have a stake in the timing of mating. Large bulls gain additional advantages by mating before their condition declines, greatly predisposing them to losing fights and mating opportunities to younger males.

One puzzling detail remains unexplained: Why do bulls often chase eager cows from rutting pits? If allowing cows to wallow ultimately improves the reproductive success of bulls, why don't bulls encourage as many cows as possible to use their pits? Field data indicated that cows are eventually exposed to the urine of bulls despite efforts by bulls to deny them access to pits. Competition for fresh urine might explain why bulls at times displace cows. Or bulls may attempt to reduce the amount of urine that cows acquire from pits in order to increase that which they gain by rubbing the bodies of bulls. Such contact would allow courtship of reluctant females and perhaps increase the probability of mating when cows are receptive.

Cessation of Feeding

The same basic approach was used to determine why large bull moose don't eat during part of the rutting season. Basic field observations framed several questions, hypotheses and their predictions followed, and more

Both cows and bulls have dewlaps or bells, but those of bulls are much more prominent.

data were obtained to test each prediction in order to best explain the purpose of this behavior.

It seems strange that large bulls would restrict their food intake just as their energy expenditures peak during the nonstop activities that accompany the rut, but that is exactly the pattern we observed. Following a summer of constant gorging on succulent leaves and twigs, bulls begin to feed less by mid-August as leaves become more fibrous and less nutritious. They use different habitats and adjust their intake of different species at this time. In my Denali study moose moved to higher elevations as the first frosts reduced the quality of certain plants such as willows. Alder shrubs have thick, fleshy leaves that are frost resistant, and moose feed heavily on them in late August. In early September large bulls suddenly stop feeding.

As with scent marking, other biologists had published hypotheses regarding appetite suppression and feeding cessation in rutting male members of the deer family. One hypothesis stated that rutting males cease feeding because rutting activities supplant the time necessary for feeding. Perhaps males that maximize time spent rutting and minimize feeding time are more successful at producing offspring than those that continue to feed. Also, reduced feeding might enhance fighting. Bulls lacking the weight and bulk normally present in their digestive tracts when they are feeding might gain speed useful in winning fights. Another hypothesis stated that the appetite is suppressed by hormonal changes or by other chemical processes that accompany rutting. Yet another idea was that failure to eat is a by-product of other processes and has no special purpose itself. Finally, reduced eating may be associated with scent marking. Odor and chemical composition of urine might be influenced by metabolic changes associated with reduced food intake and burning of stored fat and protein.

If large, rutting bulls have no time to feed, an analysis of their activity should indicate that most of their time is spent in rutting activities. If they cease to feed in order to devote all their time to the rut, bulls should time their decreased feeding to coincide with the peak of the rut in late September. Similarly, if fighting is related to intake reduction, bulls should not eat during the rut's peak, when fighting is most common. And if reduced eating and scent marking are related, bulls should not eat when rutting pits are dug and scent marking is at its peak.

Field observations indicated a much different pattern of feeding behavior for cows, small bulls, and large bulls during the autumn rutting season. Cows continued to feed during the entire rut and spent most of the time they were active each day eating. Small bulls reduced their feeding time somewhat during the rut, but large bulls stopped feeding entirely during the middle part of the rut prior to mating. They gradually resumed feeding during the peak of the rut, but they did not feed at the high rate that occurred in mid-August until the rut was over in early October. Were bulls feeding at night when we did not observe them? If so, we would have seen them chewing their cuds during the day, but we did not.

Were large bulls so busy rutting they had no time to feed? Activity budgets indicated bulls stood inattentively about 30 percent of the time they were active, and this behavior peaked during the middle of the rut when bulls ate nothing. This would have allowed them ample opportunity to feed. Something other than lack of time apparently prevented feeding.

Did bulls stop feeding to become better fighters? Most fights happened during the peak of the rut when mating occurred. Clearly it is

Bulls and cows establish signposts by rubbing bark from trees and shrubs.

much more important for bulls to win fights at this time. But bulls stopped feeding before the peak of the rut and resumed eating as the mating period began. If failure to eat was strongly related to fighting, the two behaviors should have coincided, and bulls should not have resumed feeding until the rut was over.

Were feeding cessation and scent marking in rutting pits related? The timing of these behaviors overlapped, with most of the pit digging that occurred during the middle part of the rut prior to the start of mating. This was the time when large bulls stopped feeding. Large bulls dug about 70 percent of the observed rutting pits, while yearling bulls dug none. Small bulls dug very few pits, only about 3 percent of the total we observed. Thus the bulls that stopped feeding were the ones that produced urine for scent marking, while the bulls that continued to feed produced remarkably little.

And so it appeared that bulls did not feed because some physiological mechanism prevented it, rather than because they lacked the time to eat. This was indicated not only by studying wild moose, but also by observing captives that had access to high-quality food but few opportunities to interact with other moose.

Although scent marking at rutting pits and feeding cessation are related, the exact links between these two behaviors are still unclear. Must bulls stop eating in order to produce the strong, pungent odors in their urine necessary for scent marking? When moose are food deprived during other seasons, these odors are not evident, suggesting that hormonal changes play a role during autumn. Perhaps bulls stop eating as a by-product of other processes and there is no real purpose to it. The only thing we know for certain is that all the questions are not yet answered.

Bells and Their Function

Many people who see the large, fleshy bells hanging from the chins of bull moose wonder why on earth they have these funny-looking organs. Over the years I have spoken to thousands of people about moose, and at nearly every talk someone asks about the bell. Why do they have it? What is its function? Is it used for some particular behavior? Biologists, too, have wondered about bells. My colleagues and I had the opportunity to learn more about this puzzling structure during the course of our studies at Denali.

Many large mammals have special markings, hair patches, or skin appendages. Some, like colored rump patches or prominent tails, are located at the rear of the body. Others, including contrasting colors, are located on the sides. Still others, like manes, beards, or bells, are in the neck and head region close to horns, antlers, and ears. All such structures play a role in signaling information to other animals of the same species. This may include advertising the status of an animal, or these organs may be involved in threats or displays. The prominent bell of the bull moose is one of the most obvious structures evident among members of the deer family.

Cows rub trees with their faces and necks
as they become receptive for mating.

Signposts made by moose remain prominent for months or years.

We examined two hypotheses that tried to explain the function of the bell. The first stated that bells of bulls played a role in scent marking. Bells served to absorb urine and helped transfer it to cows. The second indicated that the bell was a visual structure that advertised an animal's social rank.

The scent-marking hypothesis predicts that bulls should soak their bells with urine, and cows should contact the bells of bulls more than other parts of the body. The visual organ hypothesis predicts that dominant, high-ranking males should carry certain types of bells different from those of lower-ranking moose.

Our field observations certainly indicated that cows eagerly sought the urine that bulls deposited in rutting pits. Their excitement when bulls scent marked was obvious, as some came running from a hundred yards away to get into the pits. They also smelled and rubbed the bodies of bulls that had splashed and wallowed in the pits. Though bulls liberally labeled themselves with the odors and chemicals in their urine, we failed to observe them deliberately trying to soak their bells with urine. When they splashed in the pits, most of the mud and urine went onto the antlers and sides of their heads as they tilted them from side to side. When they wallowed, bells seldom came in contact with the pit. Mostly, bulls labeled their underbellies.

When cows approached bulls, they often touched noses while smelling each other, a form of greeting. Most of the contact cows made with bulls involved the body, rather than the head and neck. Cows contacted the bells of bulls less than expected by chance. Our observations indicated that cows were not receiving much bull urine by contacting the bells of bulls. Most of the urine they acquired came from wallowing in pits.

During the autumn rut, bulls display marked differences in rank and dominance, with the largest males clearly outranking the smaller ones. The bells of large males differ greatly from those of smaller males in size and shape. Bell characteristics and social rank are related.

And so it seemed that while bells of bulls did acquire urine, and bells could disperse odors and chemicals, there was no evidence that the function of the bells was to transfer urine to cows. We concluded that the visual role of bells in providing information about the sex, age, and social rank of bulls mainly explained their purpose. Bulls that effectively advertise themselves to other bulls as being of high rank might avoid more fights, suffer fewer injuries, and expend less energy, thereby achieving higher reproductive success. Small bulls that signal their lower rank with bells different from those of large bulls might avoid dangerous confrontations and injuries. That silly flap of skin below the chin, the bell, may play a more important role in the lives of moose than many people realize.

Signposts

We also studied the creation of signposts by moose. These are small trees that moose mark in autumn by stripping bark from trunks with either their antlers or teeth. In northern forests where moose are abundant, such

Mating is dominated by mature bulls that drive off rivals or defeat them in violent fights.

Hunting may remove most of the mature bulls from certain populations, leaving only smaller bulls to mate with cows. The long-term genetic effects of this are unknown.

trees are common, and in traditional rutting areas they can be easily spotted. The trees often die, as large areas of bark are removed from the trunk about three to six feet above ground. This is not the same as bark stripping by moose in late winter or spring, when bark is consumed as food.

Several questions guided the study. Did moose prefer certain tree species to mark? Were the marked trees distributed randomly, or were they clumped in certain areas? Did bulls and cows perform the tree marking, and did small bulls mark as commonly as large bulls? When did moose create signposts, and why did they mark trees?

Behavioral observations indicated that bulls exclusively used their antlers to scrape bark from trees. Bulls created most of the marked trees.

Cows created fewer signposts and did so by using their incisors to scrape bark from tree trunks. Cows rubbed their faces and necks on scraped trunks, often as a signal that they were ready to mate. Individuals might rub one trunk for periods up to an hour. Other females often tried to aggressively displace rivals from signposts so they could rub them. Dominant females in large groups might successfully defend posts from several other cows. We observed cows create new posts often rather than use existing ones a day or more old.

Cows and bulls differed in the times that each marked trees. Fresh signposts were rarely seen before the peak of the rut when mating occurred. Bulls first marked trees at the end of the first rutting period in early October and continued this behavior for a month or more. Medium-size bulls did most of the bark scraping. Cows started marking trees as mating began in late September and created most of their posts during the peak of the rut.

Moose often selected white spruce trees with smooth bark to rub. The trunks of other species, including willows, birch, and black spruce, were used less than expected by chance. Small trunks, rarely exceeding four to five inches in diameter, were typically selected. Marked trees were distributed randomly within rutting areas.

Males of some members of the deer family rub tree trunks with their antlers before the rut or early in the rut, apparently as a visual sign of their presence to other males. Our observation that bull moose marked trees very late in the rut likely indicates a different function. From other observations it was clear that bull moose are not territorial and therefore need not mark trees to define territory boundaries. We also observed that the largest, most dominant males created fewer signposts than less dominant animals. Might signposts by bull moose function as signals to cows rather than bulls?

After the first, main rutting period, which ends in early October, there is a second rut three weeks later. Cows that did not mate during the first rut or those that did not conceive become receptive again. Many of the largest bulls that dominated the first rut do not participate in the second. They feed intensively in an attempt to regain lost body condition before winter strikes. This allows medium-size bulls, the ones that create most of the signposts, an opportunity to mate with cows. By advertising their presence to females with large numbers of big, obvious signs, such bulls might obtain more mates.

Females rubbed not only their own posts, but also those of males. In addition to signaling readiness of cows to mate, and possibly depositing chemicals on posts from glands in the head and neck area, cows and bulls might use signposts in place of rutting pits to provide an opportunity for courtship. By early October pit digging and scent marking have waned. Rutting pits play an extremely important role in the first rutting period. In their absence during the second rut, perhaps cows and bulls seek a substitute and use posts in order to provide an arena for courtship.

Whatever their role, signposts in rutting areas are much more than idle distractions for moose in autumn. The behavior associated with them clearly has important functions.

Mating and Dominance

Before I began studying moose at Denali, I observed many of them during the autumn rutting season from airplanes. In one study I flew three or four times each week, locating radioed moose over a vast area of mountains and lowlands. This was my first opportunity to see large groups of moose during the rut. In Minnesota, where I first observed moose, such groups did not exist. The rut there consisted of one bull courting and spending time with one cow. The sex ratio in Minnesota was close to one bull per cow, but in Alaska, where there was higher mortality of bulls than cows, ratios of three or four or more cows per bull were common. There, predation, hunting, and severe winters took a heavy toll on bulls. As a result, cows without calves formed groups in autumn to ensure access to bulls for mating.

The aerial observations indicated that large bulls controlled groups of cows during the rut. Smaller bulls wandered in search of cows away from groups or hung around the edges of groups hoping to mate when the large bulls were distracted. I never saw a fight from the air, nor did I see mating. Some of the bulls showed signs that they had fought, including broken antler tines, and mating was obviously going on. The brief amounts of time that we spent circling radioed animals, often only a few minutes each day, did not allow much opportunity to see important behaviors. We therefore could not document which bulls did most of the mating or confirm the importance of preserving large males in moose populations.

Things changed when the Denali study began. Now, I was able to spend large amounts of time observing moose on the ground. I had a population of moose that had not been hunted for several decades, so there were large numbers of big bulls present. I might be able to determine which bulls were most successful at mating and which ones were not, and perhaps explain the difference. I also had radioed bulls that I could follow throughout their lives documenting changes in their mating success as they aged.

I first searched for published studies that described mating in moose but soon found that there were none. Although there were accounts of rutting behavior from a few other areas of North America, biologists had observed remarkably few instances of mating among wild moose. At Denali we would have the opportunity to observe mating and to determine the importance of size and rank to the mating success of bulls.

Despite one of the best situations in North America to observe rutting moose, it took a long time at Denali to acquire enough observations to provide meaningful results. Over a twelve-year period, we observed mating eighty-six times. Mating began as early as September 24 and continued as late as October 8. As in other areas of North America, the peak of mating for moose was centered on October 1. The rut occurred at the same time each year, evidently independent of differences in temperature or snowfall, suggesting that it was controlled by changes in day length that remained constant from year to year.

Ninety-eight percent of observed mating involved females mating with only one male. Rarely did females mate with two males, and none mated with more than two. Large males performed 88 percent of all mating; yearling males accounted for less than 2 percent. Clearly the largest, highest-ranking bulls were doing most of the mating. Field observations indicated that they accomplished this by defending cows from smaller bulls, aggressively chasing them off, and by defeating challengers in fights. The lowest-ranking animals, including yearlings that were at the bottom of the totem pole, had very little success. Even certain older males that were small for their age, or were poor fighters, could not compete with the top-ranking bulls. We observed certain bulls mate up to three times per day and estimated that some might mate up to twenty-five times per year if they possessed large groups. This was rare, however, as bulls seldom were able to control groups throughout the entire rut. Typically they were defeated in fights with rivals. Some groups had had five or more dominant

Bulls devote much time to sparring as they prepare for fights that will determine their reproductive success.

males, each in control for only a few days, by the time the rut was over.

Our results at Denali generated several questions about the importance of preserving large bulls in moose populations. In some areas hunting removes many bulls, and the ratio of cows to bulls may be ten to one. At what ratio do some cows fail to mate during the main rutting period? If many cows conceive after the main rut, is the survival of calves affected? If small bulls do most of the mating, are there unknown long-term effects? If most of the small males are successful at mating, as opposed to only a few large males, how are the genetics of the population affected? These questions are unanswered at present. Scientists often conclude their reports by noting that more research is needed. That is certainly the case here.

Sparring and Fighting

One of the first moose that I radioed at Denali was a young bull that seemed full of promise. That year he was still too young to compete well with older, larger, more experienced bulls. During autumn he spent a lot of time sparring with bulls his age, learning about fighting, and assessing the size, strength, and antlers of his opponents. The following year he was ready to begin challenging mature bulls in an attempt to mate with cows. Early that autumn we saw him fight a time or two, and later he challenged one of the largest bulls in the area. It was a mistake that cost him his life. During the fight, he broke one of his antlers at the base. His rival proceeded to inflict serious injuries on him, and four days later he was dead. This experience sparked an intense interest in me to better understand fighting by bull moose.

Moose spar and fight. Each is a distinctly different behavior. Sparring is practice fighting that bulls use to gain experience. It superficially resembles fighting, as two or more bulls engage their antlers and push each other back and forth. But fighting is far more serious and violent. At worst, sparring results in minor breakage of antlers or perhaps minor wounds inflicted by accident. Fights often result in serious injuries. At worst, fights result in death.

If sparring involves learning about fighting and about rivals, young, inexperienced bulls should participate in it more than older bulls. That is exactly what the field observations at Denali indicated. The younger bulls at times sparred to excess. Older bulls rarely sparred. If sparring is merely practice fighting, it should lack preliminary threats and displays. Again, we observed this to be the case. Bulls came together and sparred, not after lowering their ears or pawing the ground, but rather after feeding side by

Bulls fight to obtain mating rights to cows. Fights may result in serious injuries or death.

side or engaging in some other harmless behavior. Practice sparring should result in no winners or losers, and there should be no serious efforts to wound opponents. Bulls observed in the field didn't chase each other after sparring, trying to run off rivals, nor did they engage in all-out efforts to crush opponents. Sparring often consisted of little more than gentle antler contact and mild pushing. It did not escalate to fighting and did not determine dominance or rank.

Fights are another matter entirely. Bull moose are well equipped to fight. At up to sixteen hundred pounds, they are enormously powerful. Their shoulders are huge, and during the rut their neck muscles expand to twice their normal size. The skin on their foreheads is thick, providing armor against punctures by opponents. And they posses weapons and shields in the form of antlers, large, strong structures specifically designed for fighting. Antlers engage during fights, thereby allowing bulls to push

Large, dominant bulls may each fight dozens of times during their lifetimes. Those that successfully defeat rivals have high reproductive success.

and wrestle. Attached to the broad palms are sharp points that can severely wound opponents, puncturing the body, injuring eyes, or bruising muscles.

The fights we observed always involved only two opponents, never three or more as sometimes participated in sparring. On occasion young bulls fought, but most fights were between two mature bulls of approximately equal size. Prior to clashing antlers, fighting bulls engaged in intense displays and threats directed at each other, including pawing the ground, thrashing their antlers against shrubs, and displaying their bodies and antlers. Clashes were extraordinarily violent, with nothing spared in an attempt to twist an opponent's head, shove him backward, cause him to fall, and gore him. Opponents tried to gore each other whenever antlers were disengaged in a clash. Bulls in fights each sought tactical advantages, including gaining the uphill position to maximize battering effects. And there were definite winners and losers. Losers knew the dangers of remaining nearby and either left or were escorted out of the area by their rivals.

Fighting carries enormous risks, as demonstrated by the bull that broke his antler. We observed all sorts of serious injuries. Eye injuries were common. Blinded bulls obviously were handicapped, not only during the rut, but also throughout the rest of the year. Some wounds became infected, at times causing death weeks or months later. Limbs were injured, resulting in limping and reduced mobility. Injured animals fell prey to bears and wolves. Serious injuries further drained already weakened bulls and affected their survival when winter came.

Based on the number of rivals each dominant bull had, and the rate of fighting that we observed, I calculated that dominant bulls that controlled large groups might fight up to twelve times each autumn. If such bulls were dominant for three years, this suggests that the probability was extremely high that they would sustain at least one serious injury during their prime. Field observations of radioed bulls indicated that this was the case. Certain bulls were badly injured several times but recovered. Others died sooner than they might have were it not for the dangers inherent in fighting.

Why, then, should bulls put themselves through all this? Simply because in order to be successful by passing on their genes, they must defeat their rivals, control groups of cows, and mate with them. In places like Denali, with three or more cows per bull, rutting groups of up to twenty females, and about a half of all bulls being large, mature males, the competition among males was very intense. Only bulls with the size, skill, and desire to fight and win were rewarded with mating rights. Bulls were willing to risk injuries and death in order to pass on their genes.

After watching many fights and following the fates of bulls as they struggled to survive and reproduce, I greatly admire the bravery of bull moose. The ones that died taught me a lot, and I am grateful that I knew them.

They Live If They Can and Die If They Must

For many years my main professional interest was trying to understand the effects of predation by bears and wolves on moose numbers. This focus began early in my career. I had just started studying moose in Minnesota when the first of many studies of moose and wolves at Isle Royale National Park, Michigan, was published. At the University of Minnesota, where I was a graduate student, this monograph caught the attention of the wildlife biology students and staff. It certainly caught my attention. It detailed the first intensive fieldwork to document the impact of wolf predation on moose and discussed many aspects of this complex relationship. The main finding was that populations of about six hundred moose and twenty wolves could remain stable on the island over time, the moose in balance with their predators and food supply, able to sustain losses to predation by producing calves at high rates.

During the course of my career, many studies like this were completed in North America, as were predator and prey studies on various other species. But as the studies multiplied, it became clear that ecological relationships were far from simple. Although biologists today have a vastly better understanding of predation, there are still gaps in our knowledge, uncertainties, and differing interpretations of study results. And when the management of important species like moose, bears, and wolves gets intertwined with the politics of predator control, science may be misused or ignored.

Moose are large and strong, they are wary, they prefer dense cover and easy access to ponds and streams, their senses of smell and hearing are exceptionally acute, and they have great endurance, excellent speed, and remarkable agility for a large animal. All of these characteristics and many more are largely the result of the fact that for all of their evolutionary history, moose have been the prey of large, fierce, efficient predators. Predators and their prey evolve together, each developing the tools necessary to survive. Bears and wolves, the main predators of moose, evolved intelligence; strong teeth and claws; excellent eyesight, sense of smell, and hearing; and remarkable endurance and strength—all as aids in being better predators. Moose developed the ability to detect, evade, and avoid

Brown bears kill about half of the moose calves born in certain moose populations.

All of the senses of moose, including eyesight, evolved in response to the presence of several large, efficient predators that have hunted moose for thousands of years.

predators, and attained the size and skills necessary for defense. Biologists have termed this an evolutionary arms race. The end result is predators and prey that are much different animals than they would be in each other's absence.

Populations of moose have persisted over time with their predators, even though predation takes a heavy toll at times. Predation has not driven moose to extinction, and in many places moose thrive despite abundant predators. In addition, predation is not the only cause of moose mortalities. Starvation during severe winters accounts for thousands of moose deaths in certain areas. Parasites, including ticks, can cause deaths. Accidents such as breaking through ice, falls from cliffs, and drowning occur. And people account for many moose by hunting and through collisions with automobiles and trains. Despite all this, moose populations persist and in some areas reach high densities. Moose populations may sustain heavy losses and decline, only to rebound when conditions change. Even if predation reduces moose numbers, the predators themselves decline as their food supply shrinks, and eventually fewer moose are killed.

Virtually all studies of predation on large mammals have shown that predators cannot kill individual prey animals at will. Although predators may try to kill them, many prey animals simply are too clever, too strong, too defensive, or too swift to succumb. By examining the remains of prey, determining ages, detecting infirmities, and measuring body condition, biologists have determined that it is mainly the very young, the old, or the otherwise infirm animals that die at the hands of predators. There are many prey animals that by virtue of their age and physical condition are virtually immune to predation. For moose, animals aged about two to eight are in their prime and fall prey to bears and wolves only if very unlucky or debilitated by malnutrition or injuries.

On the other hand, bears and wolves kill moose calves frequently. Those less than two months old are especially vulnerable, but predators take many calves during winter as well. At times, in places where hunting and trapping of predators and prey are absent, the combined impact of predation on calves may be so severe that moose numbers decline to very low levels. Even though female moose are remarkably adept at hiding calves and are formidable defenders when discovered, wolves and bears may take a heavy toll. Calves that survive the critical first few months of life may succumb during winter when deep snow robs them of nutrition and gives wolves the advantage. But in most places most of the time, especially when bears and wolves are reduced by hunting and trapping, moose populations are able to balance losses to predation with gains from recruiting sufficient numbers of young.

In autumn moose are fat and at their seasonal peak of body condition. They spend summer feeding on high-quality food, processing huge quantities of leaves and twigs. The energy and protein extracted from the summer diet go to produce milk for calves, a new hair coat, new antlers, and vast quantities of fat, up to 250 pounds for mature males. Gone are the bony ribs, scraggly coats, and thin muscles of early summer. Rivers and ponds are still ice-free and provide escape from predators, and snow, if present, is shallow. All these things indicate that during autumn, moose are quite secure from predators compared with other seasons, when they are more vulnerable. It is difficult for a predator to kill a 1,600-pound bull moose with large, sharp-pointed antlers, capable of killing a large bear or wolf with a single kick, when the moose is not hampered by deep snow or weakened by malnutrition.

Nevertheless, some moose fall prey in autumn. Calves are still much smaller and weaker than adults and lack the experience necessary to evade predators. Some adults are old and perhaps infirm. And some males, weakened from weight loss during the mating season or injured in fights, are vulnerable. Occasionally males lock antlers during sparring or fighting and are

Brown bears kill adult moose as well as calves and at times depress moose numbers.

Gray wolves prey upon moose during all seasons of the year. Moose in their prime seldom fall prey, but young, old, or infirm animals are vulnerable to wolves.

defenseless. They may linger and starve and be eaten as carrion, or may be killed outright if discovered by predators. But during autumn, most moose escape death by predation. Their predators have a hard time making a living at this time of year and must bide their time until winter turns the tables, giving them the advantage.

During the course of my moose research, I documented many cases of predation on moose, and many more cases where moose survived to old age despite abundant predators. One study animal that we radioed was named Whitey, a tribute to the light-colored streaks in his antler velvet that were evident at a distance. He had one of the largest sets of antlers of any radioed bull and was, in his prime, probably about ten years of age. We collared him in August, just as his antlers were fully grown, and followed him during the early rutting season in September. Whitey moved long distances and used remote areas, so I couldn't see him regularly. I became suspicious when his radio signal seemed stationary for several days, so my assistants and I walked in one day to check. After a long hike, we reached the area in question. Suddenly I spotted a large mound with a big male grizzly bear on top eyeing us. Such situations are dangerous, as bears often defend their kills. Luckily, the bear just "woofed" and ran off. The mound contained Whitey's remains covered with ground debris the bear used to deter birds and other scavengers.

Moose are constantly vigilant for sights, sounds, or smells of predators.

Moose often stand their ground as wolves approach and can lash out with all four feet in self-defense.

We retreated and came back in about a week after the carcass was consumed. Little remained other than the massive antlers and skull and a few of the larger bones. As a result, we had no idea if Whitey had been injured in a fight with another bull or had some other problem that predisposed him to bear predation. He did have a broken antler tine, indicating a fight. But at times large bears are able to kill uninjured bull moose as they lose their wariness during the rut, wandering long distances in search of cows

while not eating. I have a theory that on windy nights bears are able to stalk bulls and surprise them at close range, the noise of their approach covered by the wind. If bulls run from such an encounter, bears can attack from behind and inflict fatal wounds that bulls could avoid by facing the bear head-on, using their formidable antlers as offensive weapons. I have found bear-killed bull moose, including Whitey, during autumn quite often after windstorms.

In contrast to Whitey, Spinepalm was another large, radioed bull that would have been easy prey for bears but survived for an extended period. Just as he lost his antler velvet in late August and the rutting season began, Spinepalm sickened, apparently as a result of digestive system problems. He did what sick moose usually do, finding some dense cover and remaining there. I checked on him regularly during the following month as his condition deteriorated. His vast fat reserves were the only thing keeping him alive. The area he inhabited, only an acre or two in size, must have been ripe with moose odors, and I saw one

Cows with young calves may chase wolves off or stand their ground and kick predators that come near.

Calves less than eight weeks old are vulnerable to wolves and bears and may be killed at high rates despite the defensive capabilities of their mothers.

bear nearby that apparently left the moose alone. After about six weeks, Spinepalm was perhaps only a few days away from death. Some biologist colleagues of mine watched as a pack of wolves discovered and consumed him. It was largely irrelevant at that point whether predators or starvation was the proximate cause of death, but I was surprised that a moose in that state survived as long as he did in the presence of many bears, some of which are always alert to the chance for a moose kill.

Female moose can live to twenty-one years of age, but males seldom live beyond fifteen. Moose older than twenty are the equivalents of hundred-year-old humans. Three of my radioed moose lived to advanced age in the presence of bears and wolves. Two were cows that lived to age nineteen. One even produced a calf in her final year. One bull was smaller than aver-age and lacked the size necessary to compete with more dominant males during the rut. He spent his time in autumn wandering widely in search of cows in remote places away from most other bulls. When he was seventeen, truly an ancient bull, he wandered outside his traditional area and was shot by a hunter. This old bull was very thin and carried numerous scars. These three moose all lived in areas where bears and wolves preyed heavily on

In early autumn mature bulls are in peak condition and have formidable defenses against predators.

Severe winters with deep snow result in moose starvation and make moose more vulnerable to predation.

moose, but they survived to very old age, whether through luck or skill or superior genes. They also had to survive many other things, including severe winters with deep snow, a hazard that in the long run, in most areas, is much more significant for moose than are predators.

Accounts of individual animals surviving in the presence of predators are interesting, but what is known about moose populations in areas where bears and wolves thrive? Are moose numbers reduced to very low levels or do populations persist, fluctuating up and down over time? One of the best places in the world to determine this is Denali National Park and Preserve in central Alaska. Here moose, their predators, and the land they occupy have been protected for eight decades. Charles Sheldon, a naturalist, visited the area that would later become the park nearly a hundred years ago and found moose abundant. Of course, moose had occupied this area for thousands of years prior to his visit. Sheldon's descriptions of moose habitat closely match the patterns seen today, because in this subarctic location, the plant associations are very stable. The park was established in 1917 but not fully protected from market hunting until moose numbers were greatly reduced. Under full protection, moose increased in the presence of bears and wolves and reached high levels by 1970. They then declined, in part from heavy bear predation, until numbers stabilized by about 1990. Even after the decline moose were still relatively common.

Despite tales of north-country residents that bears and wolves decimate moose populations, the lesson from Denali is clearly that moose populations persist, at times reaching moderate levels. But predators in such environments do keep moose populations somewhat in check. In many North American locations lacking predators, moose may increase to high densities, eat most of their food supply, and decline greatly during severe winters. Even at Isle Royale National Park, where bears are absent, moose have increased, starved, and declined at times, despite the presence of wolves. It takes both bears and wolves to significantly and

Moose skulls may persist for many years.

Ponds, lakes, and streams provide means of escape for moose pursued by predators during the ice-free seasons.

Moose persist in Denali National Park at moderate densities despite the presence of bears and wolves.

persistently stabilize moose numbers, but despite this effect, moose populations in most places do just fine coexisting with their predators.

Why is it, then, that controversial bear and wolf control programs are occasionally proposed in northern areas to increase moose populations? At times, especially after severe winters or habitat losses, moose populations decline and hunting suffers. There are still places where people depend on moose meat as an important food source, and poor hunting means significant hardships for them. But if predator control is considered, it is good public policy to ensure that it is preceded by good science to be certain that predators are really the problem, that predator reduction will result in more moose, and that predator reduction is cost-effective. In addition, the methods of control must be humane and accepted by the public. The worst possible situation is to implement predator control where it is unneeded, unworkable, or unnecessary, and where it is based on poor science. Wolf control zealots at times ignore or distort science to advance their agenda.

The resulting programs, based largely on politics and strong emotions, may become institutionalized and difficult to terminate even if proven to be ineffective.

Many people object to predator control on principle. They think that while wolves and bears are important predators, they have great intrinsic values of their own. Labeling them as predators diminishes their status. Many believe that, for example, large-scale aerial wolf-shooting programs with helicopters is wildlife management gone awry. It seems to them that moose management in the vast wilderness areas of the Far North can never be the same as white-tailed deer management in Midwestern farming areas. Should not moose hunters value wilderness experiences, including the chance to see wolves and their signs or hear them howling, as much as actually getting a moose? Decisions on implementing predator control programs are fundamentally matters of public policy, not biology. Biologists can only provide advice on the details of the programs and describe options. The public, through the political process, must decide whether or not to proceed. We can only hope that, in the end, some measure of wisdom prevails.

Cows with young calves often remain near water bodies that provide means of escape from predators.

Cow and Calf

On a late April day in 1980 my assistant and
I traveled to Denali National Park in central
Alaska to begin fieldwork on an ecological study
of moose. I had visited the park for the first time several
years earlier to camp, enjoy the wonderful mountain
scenery, and observe the moose, caribou, wolves, bears,
and mountain sheep that inhabited this vast area of subarctic land. Before moving to Alaska and working there as
a wildlife biologist, I read about the park and about some
of the biological studies done there. My first visits to
Denali confirmed my expectations. The park was a special
place, and I felt fortunate to live close enough that I could
drive there often and experience its environment, both
near the park road and in the backcountry. But it was
especially exciting when I had the opportunity to propose
a long-term moose study to the park staff. I had worked
with moose in Minnesota and in other areas of Alaska
and recognized that Denali offered the chance to do
research that couldn't be done elsewhere. I wanted a place
with road access to keep costs down, an abundant population of moose, a chance to observe wild moose at close
range without disturbing them, and a place where moose,
their predators, and the habitat were largely unaffected by
people. Denali met these criteria, and I was overjoyed
when my proposal was approved. Now it was time to
begin studies of moose behavior, population changes over
time, and predation on moose by wolves and bears.

The first step in these studies was to capture some
bulls and cows and equip them with collars containing
small radio transmitters. Each collar had its own radio
frequency so we could locate individual moose with
antennas and portable receivers. We could drive the park
road, stop at intervals, listen for signals, get bearings, and
walk to the animal. By having radioed moose, we could
learn a tremendous amount about their lives, from the

areas they occupied to how long they lived. We could study their mating behavior, the survival of their calves, what they ate, and numerous other things that were unknown or poorly studied. I especially wanted to learn about the lives of individual moose as they aged. Moose can live twenty or more years, and invaluable data can be obtained by following radioed animals for much of their lives. But first we had to capture moose.

In late April the first signs of spring appear at Denali. Days are becoming long and temperatures are warm enough to melt a little snow. Willow plants produce catkins, the shrub equivalent of flowers. Snow has settled and crusted as warm days and cold nights act upon it. It may be another five weeks before the snow is completely gone, but the end of winter is unmistakably near. For their part, moose respond to these seasonal changes by shaking off some of the lethargy of winter, feeding more, and interacting a little with other moose as they jointly use productive patches of food plants. As snow settles, it exposes low-growing shrubs for the first time in several months. Moose eagerly seek these as the small, nutritious twigs are much superior to the tall, coarse stems available in midwinter. Antlers of bulls have already sprouted. Cows are heavy with calves that are only about a month away from being born.

We were able to drive about fifteen miles into the park, so my assistant and I cruised the road looking for moose we could capture. In one area of scattered spruce trees and tall shrubs typical of moose habitat in this area,

Part of my moose study area in Denali National Park, where research has been conducted since 1980.

White-colored moose are extraordinarily rare. This cow had brown eyes and was not an albino.

we located a group of a dozen or more cows and bulls. We gathered our gear and set out to dart and collar the first of many moose that I would eventually study in the park. In places the snow was still thigh-deep, and we broke through the crust often. Most moose at Denali are very tolerant of people. We were able to approach them easily to within the range of our dart gun. It was then a matter of selecting, darting, and collaring animals for several days in three different areas, capturing each moose in turn and ensuring that they all recovered. It went smoothly and the study was off to a good start.

One of the first moose that we collared was an adult cow. She really was not much different than the others, of average size, perhaps a bit darker in color than most, with a small, dark spot on one shoulder. Bulls are often easily identifiable, especially when they have antlers. Even when they don't, bulls have distinctive bells, and their ears are often uniquely split or notched from fighting. But cows look much the same, differing only in size, color, and bell configuration. The radioed cow appeared to be a young moose, perhaps five or six years old. Her teeth were not very worn, signaling that she was relatively young. I named her Missy and looked forward to following her around for several years learning the details of her life.

Missy roamed the eastern part of Denali close to the park road. During summer I kept track of the calves she produced and monitored their survival. For the most part, Missy's calves died young, many likely killed by

These calves, only a few minutes old, were born to a radioed cow named Missy that was part of a long-term moose study in Denali National Park.

grizzlies during a time when bears accounted for the deaths of more than half the moose calves produced. Wolves also took a few calves, and some died from congenital problems, accidents, and all the other hazards that young calves face. Missy, like most of the moose cows in the park, had poor success in rearing calves.

During the early years of the study, in summer we were mostly trying to learn about feeding by moose. My assistants observed moose at close range making note of the plant species they ate and the rates and sizes of the bites they took of leaves and twigs. We also followed moose for twenty-four-hour periods, recording their activity in an attempt to estimate the time they spent feeding. Missy was one of several moose involved in these studies. She was tolerant of people and provided us the opportunity to learn the details of what and where moose ate, and to attempt to explain why they behaved as they did.

I followed Missy for several years as she participated in the autumn mating season or rut. Cows spend most of the summer alone if they lose their calves, or they may briefly accompany other cows. They have no interest in bulls until the rut begins in late August. Then there is a month of preliminaries before mating begins. During a two-week period in late September and early October, there is frenzied activity as bulls compete for cows, and most of the adult cows conceive. Moose in the Far North form rutting groups of up to twenty or more cows and one dominant bull. Most of the cows without calves join such groups. Individual moose are often faithful to traditional rutting areas. Missy led me to her rutting area each year for several years, and I began to learn the details of mating, fighting, scent marking, and all the other behaviors that occur during the autumn rutting season.

During the peak of the rut one year, I tracked Missy to an area we called the Hot Spot in honor of all the moose that normally lived there.

It was a large patch of scattered spruce and tall willows, some reaching four feet above my head. In autumn it was one of several traditional rutting areas we studied, drawing twenty or more moose each year as the rut unfolded. Missy had been there before, but it was her second choice. She preferred another place about two miles away that attracted fewer moose. It was late September and about six inches of snow covered the ground as I walked uphill following the radio signal. Missy was at the edge of the willows and several other females were nearby, but I couldn't easily count them in the dense cover. I could hear a bull about a hundred yards off as he thrashed his antlers against shrubs and vocalized with croaks, a peculiar sound that bulls make during the rut. As I moved through the willows looking for moose, I suddenly saw a cow unlike any I had seen before. She was white. Not pure white, but nearly so. Her eyes were brown, indicating that she was not albino, and she had a few small, colored marks on her sides. I was astounded. There were reports of white moose in Denali going back several decades, but I had never seen such an animal and had not heard of recent sightings. She was very tolerant of me, and I spent a couple of hours with her taking photos. This was one of my most memorable moments with moose, spent in the company of an extraordinarily rare animal. It was six years before I saw her again for the last time. I can vividly recall how beautiful she was and how the other moose seemed to pay no attention at all to her special color.

Cows lick their newborn calves free of birth fluids shortly after birth.

One autumn I agreed to guide a television crew as they filmed moose behavior. Denali not only provides researchers with unparalleled opportunities to observe moose, but also provides film crews with footage they cannot get elsewhere. A cameraman and I spent several days filming rutting behavior before the host of the show arrived from England. He was accompanied by his own cameraman, who had an assistant, plus a soundman and a producer. They wanted to film a sequence where the host talked on camera about fighting while a bull stood in the background. My general rule is to keep such crews to three people or less, so after we had trimmed the staff, we walked a short distance from the road to Missy and her rutting group of seven cows and one large bull. The bull was busy tending cows and chasing off a couple small males, and it was difficult to set up the shot. Finally we began, with the camera rolling and the host talking. Suddenly the bull decided to chase off one of his smaller rivals standing behind us and came on the run. The Englishman tried to run but stumbled and fell. He couldn't believe moose could move that fast. After that, the host was badly frightened and felt that moose disliked him. The bull went back to tending his cows, and the crew eventually filmed the sequence, but the host could barely take his eyes off the bull long enough to look at the camera. Missy stood by the entire time perhaps wondering what all the fuss was about.

After following Missy for ten years, prying into all the details of her life, I tracked her one spring as she returned from her winter range about thirty miles north of the park. Some Denali moose migrate in early winter, seeking habitats with less snow and more food in the lowlands. Missy had left the park in early December the previous year as snow buried the

In areas where predation is heavy, one or both twin calves may perish.

smaller shrubs and raised the energy costs of moose breaking trail through it. Now she returned to the same area that she used each summer to bear her calves and feed on the lush foliage found in the willow and alder thickets. The winter that year was not severe, and Missy had survived it well. She lacked the bony ribs and hips that moose have after losing a lot of weight from struggling with deep snow. In fact, she appeared fat, as her belly was distended. But she was not fat; rather, she was very pregnant and would soon give birth.

I was locating my collared cows daily during the time they gave birth, determining how many calves they produced and monitoring their survival. On a bright, warm spring day I followed Missy's radio signal to a small patch of

Calves that survive the first few critical months of life weigh about three hundred pounds by early autumn.

spruce trees. She heard me coming as she had many times before, preceded by sounds from the beeping radio receiver, and she soon realized that I wasn't a bear. I didn't know if she had given birth yet, but cow moose with young calves can be dangerous, so I cautiously moved near until I saw her lying in a small opening. She was licking a newborn calf only a few hours old, and its twin was lying nearby. Both were alert and seemed healthy. Moose calves are remarkably precocious. They stand within minutes of birth. Mothers clean them of birth fluids and eat the afterbirth, a behavior that helps minimize the chances that predators will detect them. I spent about an hour with Missy and her latest set of calves, watching as they nursed for the first time.

Each day I checked the approximate location of my collared cows by radio signal bearings, and every two or three days I visited them to see if the calves were well. For nearly three weeks I watched Missy's calves nurse and rest, occasionally playing by butting their heads or dashing about. At this age they sometimes rested as Missy fed some distance off. She trusted me enough that I could be near the calves, unlike some cows that aggressively protect their calves from everything they think is a threat. By being close, I was able to tell that one calf was a male, the other a female. The calves were feeding on green leaves themselves, at times watching Missy feed and imitating her choices. They were well on their way to getting a good start in life. Their mother had experience raising calves and took good care of them.

Cows typically remain close to their birth sites for up to a month, trying to remain inconspicuous. If they move, they increase the chances that predators will detect them. It's better to stay put for a while, even when food supplies run low. If predators discover them and kill one or more calves, cows normally move long distances away. When radio signals indicated such movements, I located the cows to see the results. One morning Missy's signals indicated that she was about a mile from where she had spent the previous three weeks. I found her in a small stream with only the female calf. This suggested that a predator, most likely a bear, had killed the male, but I could not be certain. Later I visited the birth site and found evidence that a bear indeed had taken the male. I found the intact skin, attached leg bones and hooves, and a few scattered bones typical of a bear kill. Would the same fate claim the female calf and repeat the pattern of previous years, or could Missy evade predators and finally rear a calf to adulthood?

My Denali fieldwork schedule at that time involved leaving in mid-June and returning in mid-August to spend the autumn observing the rut. Over the summer I thought about Missy and wondered if her calf survived. When I returned in August the park was much different than in late June. Summer was rapidly ending. Within days green leaves would become red or yellow, and cold nights would usher in all the changes that autumn brings. On my first day back I tracked Missy to an area she had used many times before, not far from the park road near a place we called the Dwarf Birch Meadow. When I finally saw her she appeared alone, but then I saw her calf standing about fifty yards off. This was no skinny, forty-pound baby, but a three-hundred-pound preteen calf. Gone were the reddish brown coat and delicate features. This calf resembled a miniature adult. As I moved near, she took her cue from Missy and ignored me. I'm sure she recalled seeing me two months earlier and could tell the difference between me and other large animals that might harm her.

I named the calf Junior Miss, or JM for short. That autumn I spent a lot of time with Missy and JM, trying to learn some things about how they spent their time compared with how Missy lived during prior years when she had no surviving calves. Would she remain apart from rutting groups and be courted by lone bulls, or would she take JM to a group and seek a mate there? In late August it was too early to tell, but Missy avoided all other moose at that time as she and her calf spent their days mainly feeding and resting. Missy used the same home range and the same feeding areas as she had previously. JM was still nursing but at a much reduced level, and now fed on leaves and twigs nearly as long as her mother. They seldom were more than a hundred yards apart while feeding, and they often rested within a few feet of each other. Calves at this age don't play much. Their mothers often refuse to play if the calves try. But mothers do lick and nurture their calves, mostly after a nursing bout. Mainly, the job of a cow moose is to be alert to any indications of trouble. This almost always comes in the form of predators. Moose are incredibly well equipped

During the rut cows with calves often seek remote spots away from other moose. Bulls travel widely and court these females when they find them.

to see, hear, or smell predators, and cows with calves know how important it is to use those senses to their full potential.

During one of the days I was with them, Missy led her calf about a half mile to a mineral lick. Moose use licks mainly to gain sodium by drinking water in muddy pools that form at the ground's surface. This particular lick had evidently been used for centuries and had trails leading to it that were a foot or more deep, worn by thousands of moose feet moving toward and away from this important place. I often saw other moose using this lick. When my cow and calf arrived at the lick, there was another cow there. Missy ran her off while JM smelled the pools and the dirt banks and sipped a little water. After about thirty minutes there sampling water at two or three sites, Missy led her calf back to their feeding area. JM now knew the location of the lick and could return there in the future as an adult.

By mid-September bulls were digging rutting pits, marking them with smelly urine and then splashing and smearing the mud-urine mixture on their bodies. Cows, too, eagerly wanted to mark themselves with this scent as part of the complex process of priming their reproductive systems for mating. I had observed this behavior many times but seldom had the chance to see a calf's reaction to a pit. Missy one day had a suitor, a young male not quite large enough to compete with the mature bulls but plenty capable of digging well-scented pits. As I watched one afternoon, he produced a fine pit, and after using it himself, he waited as Missy cautiously moved in. Once there, she vigorously wallowed in the pit, getting up and lying down several times. I'm sure this was JM's first experience with a rutting pit, and she seemed very unsure about it. After Missy left the pit, JM went to it, smelled its contents, and wallowed there too. But she was just curious, as young animals of all sorts are prone to be. Her reproductive tract would not need priming for another two years.

Missy and JM moved to the head of a small valley in late September and stayed there during the peak of the rut when bulls and cows mated. It was an out-of-the-way place where most cows did not go during the rut. Certain cows with calves seek such places, perhaps to shelter calves from all the craziness that happens in the rutting groups. I learned that cows used places like this while flying helicopter surveys during the rut to census moose. Surveys were done after fresh snow, as moose and their tracks are then visible. While searching drainages from the air, I often found cows with calves tucked away in isolated valleys, at times far removed from the nearest rutting group. We sometimes followed single sets of moose tracks from the air for miles. They invariably were made by bulls wandering widely, searching remote places for receptive cows. Missy's spot was a long way from the road, and I was spending most of my time observing groups, so I didn't document whether Missy mated that year. One or more bulls probably found and courted her, but she was now an old female and may have skipped mating after expending the energy it took to raise JM.

Bulls may find cows with calves early in the rut and remain with them until mating occurs.

I left the park in early October after the rut ended and didn't return until the following May. Missy had again spent the winter out of the park but had migrated back before my own northward migration brought me there. I was anxious to see if JM had survived the winter and was very pleased to find her alive and well. She looked much the same as she had the previous fall, but her coat was faded a bit and more gray. Most yearlings have a kind of mouse gray color with a light shoulder spot. They also have shorter muzzles than adults and are only about half the size of their mothers. After a very close, protective, yearlong relationship, cows that are pregnant drive off their offspring just prior to giving birth. I couldn't tell if Missy was pregnant but thought she might be, so I watched for signs of aggression toward JM. Missy never showed any hostility toward JM that spring, and there was no evidence that she gave birth. She either had failed to mate or didn't conceive. As a result, she and JM remained together. I had observed other cows that followed this pattern, staying with their yearlings a few more months but separating from them by autumn.

Some older females with calves may avoid bulls and fail to mate for one or more years.

I again left the park in mid-June and returned two months later. Another autumn rutting season was at hand. Missy and JM were still

During severe winters cow moose may die, leaving behind their offspring to fend for themselves.

together, and the bond between them was as strong as ever. They spent the rut away from most other moose, but there were suitors that courted Missy. Female yearlings at Denali don't generally mate but do show interest in bulls. I saw JM approach two different bulls in late September, carefully coming near to smell their antlers and flanks, but the bulls had no interest in her. There was no evidence that Missy mated that year, a fact that didn't surprise me given her advanced age.

The following spring, when JM was two, I fully expected that she and Missy would be separated and I'd never again recognize the young female. I had never heard of a case where a cow kept her offspring for two years. But there they were on my first day back, feeding on willows near each other on the bank of a small stream. Two months later they were still together, and I was even more surprised. By then JM was nearly the size of Missy. She was a fine young female approaching maturity. She and her mother were still firmly bonded, as Missy demonstrated one day by licking JM for several minutes. JM was two but not too old to be nurtured. In late August I radioed JM, the first offspring of a radioed cow I collared at Denali. I was a little worried that Missy would defend JM from me when the drug took effect, but she did not. Having been recollared several times herself, perhaps she accepted the inevitability of it.

The rutting season was on schedule that autumn until a blizzard in mid-September dumped three feet of snow on the eastern part of the park. Temperatures dropped and winter set in. It was the earliest winter anyone could recall. The rut was disrupted as traditional areas were abandoned and moose moved to lower elevations. Some left the park as they began migrating to wintering areas. My study was also disrupted. I could barely get around in the deep snow. I did track Missy and JM until late September, when they disappeared out of range of my radio receiver.

More snow fell in December and it was one of the worst winters on record. Many moose starved. The following spring I found a third of my radioed moose dead, by far the highest proportion in the study's history. Missy was one of those that perished. I found her collar amidst a pile of hair and a few bones about five miles from her last location the previous September. Scavengers left few remains, and I couldn't determine the cause of death, but she probably was simply overwhelmed by the deep snow and lack of food.

JM survived that terrible winter without her mother. Young female moose are amazingly hardy and often survive the worst of conditions. I found JM near one of the park's campgrounds in mid-May, and she looked to be in surprisingly good condition. Two weeks later I located her in a dense spruce patch close to the campground with a single newborn calf, born nearly on JM's third birthday. This was her first calf and she reacted nervously toward me, unsure that I would be as harmless to the calf as I was to her. Each time I saw the calf over the next two weeks, I wondered if this new, fresh face would survive to represent a third generation of Misses. But that autumn JM was alone. The odds of her first calf surviving were slim. Moose cows must learn how to be good mothers, and gaining experience takes time.

My fieldwork schedule over the next ten years was the same as before, monitor birth and survival of calves in spring and observe the rut in autumn. Following the birth of her first calf, JM produced calves each year. None survived longer than three months. I documented that predation accounted for some. One had congenital problems and lived only four days. Many died while I was gone from the park during summer, and their mortality causes were simply unknown.

JM had calves in a wide variety of locations, and I learned a lot from some of the things she experienced. One birth site was on the bank of a large river. She and her calf bedded in an open place a few yards from the rushing water, and I spent several days watching to see if one of several grizzly bears that used the valley as a travel corridor would find her. It was early June, and at that time there is enough light to see the entire night. I spent two nights on the opposite bank, but nothing happened except for incessant attacks by an abundant crop of mosquitoes. The third night I dozed off a couple of times but awoke at 2 A.M. to see a bear moving upstream about two hundred yards away. JM and the calf moved into the river as the bear came as close as it could get on the bank and glared at the moose. JM had her hackles up and was ready to fight if the bear came into the water. But after several minutes the bear moved on. The moose remained in the river another fifteen minutes until the coast was clear. The calf was wet and cold and had a hard time climbing the steep bank, but it scrambled out after a time and nursed vigorously.

During a different spring JM's birth site was on a hillside in a featureless area of low shrubs. The valley at the hill's base contained Hogan Creek. I called this place a death trap for young calves, as none of the calves I saw there in previous years survived. Several bears hunted the valley each spring and were efficient at finding calves. One morning I arrived to see a bear with her yearling cub eating one of JM's calves near the birth site. There were moose and bear tracks on the dusty road, and I spotted the other calf lying near the road about four hundred yards from the bears. In the confusion of the chase, the calf and its mother had become separated. JM's radio signal indicated that she was about one mile away. The bears finished eating and left the area that afternoon. The calf never moved. That evening the calf arose and began crying out. Moose calves utter a

In the Far North deep snow and low temperatures may occur during the peak of the rut in early October.

Mature bull and cow moose often return to traditional rutting areas each autumn.

loud bleating sound when distressed, and this calf clearly wanted its mother. This went on for thirty minutes, and I expected to see a bear respond, but JM heard the calls and came running over a hill to reunite with her surviving calf. I wasn't sure which moose seemed happier, JM or the calf.

Still another incident with bears occurred as JM and her twins were spooked from a hillside one spring afternoon. They moved downhill to the park road and trotted along the shoulder for about two miles before entering a patch of spruce trees. On the way, several cars, trucks, and buses passed by, but the moose stuck to the road shoulder and kept moving. I saw this kind of event dozens of times over the years involving many different moose. Cows are able to evade bears this way, as bears are less tolerant than moose of roads and traffic.

After JM produced calves for several years, she learned that I was no threat to them and allowed me to be very close. Her birth site one year was near Park Headquarters, and when the calves were a week old, JM moved them to a triangular patch of willows behind the Park Service buildings. The park's dog kennels housed thirty or more sled dogs nearby, and demonstrations took place there for visitors three times a day. Large

buses discharged up to two hundred people, and some of them walked near JM and her calves bedded in the willows. Other moose had used this place nearly every spring and some were aggressive. A cow and her calf disrupted the dog demonstrations several times one year and would charge anyone in the area. But JM was a mellow moose and caused no trouble. She was easily accessible while in this area, and I spent several hours each day in the willows observing. When the calves played, they would chase each other in large loops, running at top speed. Several times they nearly ran into me, and one once tried to get me to play. This was a rare treat, to be with young, wild moose calves that were full of energy and life. There were only two other cows over the years that trusted me enough to allow it.

During autumn when she was a young adult, JM moved over a larger area than I expected. Missy had restricted her rutting movements to a swath of spruce forest that included a traditional rutting area. JM spent time there too, but often left to roam farther west into an area more open and hilly that supported fewer moose. Young moose are like young people; they lack experience, make mistakes, and take a while to understand how to function well with others. Older moose are often dominant over younger ones. For example, I observed older cows at rutting pits driving off younger ones, reserving the first opportunity to wallow in the fresh urine of bulls for the dominant females. Older females with experience handling the extreme social tensions of the rut were more calm than younger animals that often were unsure how to react. JM needed time to learn all she needed to know about the complex events surrounding the rut. While young, she avoided the larger rutting groups most of the time, preferring instead to join smaller groups of four or five animals.

By the time she was seven years old, JM had settled on a rutting area that she returned to by mid-September each autumn. It was not the same area her mother used, but was about four miles farther west where the largest rutting groups in my study area formed. By this time the moose population had declined sharply, and groups of thirty or more animals no longer occurred. But groups of about fifteen to twenty still occupied this site during many years at the peak of the rut. Although still young, JM was now able to take her place in the group and interact well with the other cows and bulls as they went through the annual process of rutting, participating in all the rituals of moose behavior.

I documented the dynamics of JM's rutting group each year, monitoring the loyalty of cows, the stability of numbers as the rut peaked, and turnover in the dominant bulls. Early in September JM and some of the other cows might be several miles away in the areas where they spent the

Autumn moose habitat in eastern Denali National Park, where a moose named Missy and her daughter JM roamed for more than two decades.

summer. They began to interact with bulls at that time, but any bonds they established were brief and quickly broken. By midmonth JM moved to her traditional rutting area, and the group of moose there became quite stable. A few cows might yet come and go, but most stayed, as did the dominant bull. There was a constant parade of other bulls, big and small, and fights at the peak of the rut determined the main bull in charge. Turnover in bulls was common, and some years four or five different bulls in succession won and lost control of the group.

JM experienced a lot of different bulls during the time she was part of this group. One year a bull with an abnormal antler was there in mid-September. Rather than one main beam, his left antler had two. During his first fight, most of that antler broke, and he lost the fight and his control of the group before mating began. Another year a small, energetic bull controlled the group, defeating larger bulls in fights mainly through sheer

determination. After the first week of mating he had worn down somewhat, and a larger bull appeared and took control. Yet another bull was large and confident. He won his first few fights easily but then started to limp on a rear leg. Mating was at a peak then, and other bulls that perhaps had lost their groups were coming around to challenge the king. The limp got worse, and when a large rival appeared, the king departed during the preliminary threats rather than risk serious injuries. JM and the other cows mated with whichever male was in control of the group when they were receptive. Cow moose don't actually choose their mates. Rather, they choose particular rutting groups to join, and large, dominant bulls fight to obtain mating rights to the group.

As I write this, it has been nearly twenty-three years since I first radioed Missy. Her daughter, JM, was also collared. She is now thirteen years old and still wanders the spruce forests of Denali National Park. Last autumn, when I saw her last, I thought back on all the days I spent with her and her mother, observing the births and deaths of their offspring and watching them participate in the autumn rut. They were both very patient with me and let me enter their world. From them I gained more insight into what it means to be a moose than I ever thought possible. In the process I hope I didn't distract them too much in their constant struggle to survive and reproduce.

Large bulls rest when they can during the rut to conserve energy.

Death of a Warrior

Over a decade ago on a snowy day in early October, a bull moose I named Big Boy died in the Savage River country of Denali National Park. He was a warrior who fought and won against many other bulls during his life. I didn't see the battle that resulted in his death, but I'm sure he fought it as he did the others, with skill, strength, and courage. As part of a moose research project, he taught me a lot during the six years I knew him, and upon his death I reflected on what it means to be a moose, how difficult a moose's life can be, and how exceptional animals like him survive until the end despite the odds.

During his prime, Big Boy wore a radio collar that allowed us to identify and locate him daily as we studied the moose rut each year from August to October. We followed about twenty collared bulls and cows each year, learning about the areas they used, their traditions, their choice of mates, the behaviors they used, and how these things varied from year to year depending on changes in the environment and weather. Earlier, I had become interested in fighting among bulls after another collared bull broke off an antler in a fight and died from his injuries. The vast majority of fights did not result in serious injury or death, so I wanted to learn much more about fighting to determine who won and who lost, and try to understand why. When I first saw Big Boy several years later, I knew from his size and bearing that he could help me in my quest.

Denali is one of the best places on earth for observational studies of moose. Prior to working there, I was an "airplane biologist." Like most of my colleagues, I spent a lot of time in the backseat of a Super Cub radio-tracking moose, mainly collecting data on their locations, associates, and mortality, but seldom seeing much of their behavior. At Denali a whole new world opened to

Autumn is the mating season for moose. Bulls risk serious injuries and death as they battle for mating rights to cows.

me, the chance to be with moose on the ground at close range as they did everything a moose does from mating to giving birth. Here most moose ignored me as they went about their lives, and in a few months I learned far more about what it means to be a moose than I had learned from the air during several years.

Those who know little about moose, or any wild species for that matter, may wrongly assume that all individuals are pretty much alike, stamped out like clones as a result of similar adaptations to the same environment by long-dead ancestors. As a young wildlife biologist, I underestimated how much animals differed. It was not until I began to study individual moose closely in Denali that I realized moose are highly variable in nearly all regards. Some bulls are much larger than others. Some have massive antlers. Certain cows are successful at raising calves; others lose them year after year. During severe winters, some moose know where to go and what to do to survive, while others starve. These differences apply to nearly every visible aspect of their shape, form, and behavior, as well as to the invisible things like physiology and metabolism. In short, some moose are much better than others at surviving and passing on their genes. For bulls the bottom line of success is the ability to win fights, avoid injuries, and mate with many cows.

I didn't know Big Boy as a "child" or a "teenager." Was his mother smart or just lucky to raise a calf when about 85 percent of all calves at Denali die, many from predation, during their first few months of life? Was he smart or just lucky to survive the critical months following separation from his mother after a year of her care? How quickly did he learn the rules of moose society during the rut as a yearling or two year old when he was at the bottom of the pecking order, pushed around by the larger bulls and spurned by the older cows? I could never know these things, having first collared him as a seven-year-old coming into his prime.

At seven he was fully grown and about as large as bull moose get, about sixteen hundred pounds. Most other bulls in the area were smaller, and none that year carried larger antlers. Big interior Alaska bulls grow antlers spanning sixty-five inches, with a few exceeding seventy inches. Big Boy's antlers not only had a wide spread, but also had great mass, wide palms, and long points. Along with everything else, he was handsome. Some bulls have scarred faces, rough coats, potbellies, or other unattractive features. Big Boy was sleek and unscarred, with a long, full bell hanging from his chin, an Errol Flynn sort of moose with a personality to match.

But appearance and size alone are not enough to ensure success at fighting. Like human boxers, bull moose need a host of traits to be winners. Size is important, but speed, strength, agility, and endurance also count. Fighters must have ambition and motivation to train hard for years, sacrificing things that might harm their careers. And the best fighters have a rare combination of courage, confidence, and brains that carries them through the most difficult bouts when others quit. Only a few humans become heavyweight champions, and only a few bull moose have what it takes to be dominant over their rivals. As I would later learn, Big Boy had the right stuff.

Fights among bull moose are truly spectacles of nature. They begin as two bulls advance toward each other, at times from several hundred yards away, each walking stiffly, tilting his antlers from side to side. This gives each bull time to see the other, to determine his body and antler size, age, and condition, and to assess his chances at winning against this particular rival. As they reach each other, they perform threats and displays of intimidation. Often one bull will soon turn and run, having decided against actual combat. If both persist, there comes a mighty clash of antlers that people can hear a mile away. For a few minutes both bulls push with all

Big Boy was the dominant bull in one area of Denali National Park for several years. Each year he controlled a large group of cows.

Fights are violent contests. They may last a few minutes or several hours as each bull tries to defeat his opponent.

their strength, each trying to gain the advantage. Long fights may last several hours and involve twenty or more clashes before one bull is defeated and runs off, but the contest is usually decided quickly. The battle scene of a long fight is littered with broken small trees, torn-up brush, and bits of hair gouged out by trees or antlers. Wounds are common. Rarely, bulls are killed outright if they lose their footing and are severely gored.

Why do moose risk their lives in such violent battles? They do it for the chance to control and mate with a group of cows, to be successful breeders. In the North, moose form rutting groups consisting of several cows, one dominant bull, and a series of other bulls that may challenge the leader. With few exceptions, the cows mate with the dominant bull, simply because he defends them from other males. For smaller or younger rivals, intimidation is sufficient. Dominant bulls are kept very busy threatening and chasing off these smaller pests. But for serious rivals, only fighting will determine who will control the group. During the peak of the rut, the ruler of a large group may fight three or more times a day. Under the constant pressure of mating, fighting, and intimidating lesser bulls, dominants rarely keep control of a group for long.

In places like Denali where hunting does not remove older bulls, young bulls spend the first five or six years of their lives in training. Some will have everything it takes to be dominant; others will not. Some of the bulls I collared over the years were reproduction losers. Chip and Buddy were smaller than average, with antlers that barely spanned sixty inches. Other bulls were successful at times despite their small size because they had good fighting skills or exceptional courage and patience. But Chip and

Yearling bulls are too small and inexperienced to be successful in mating with cows as older bulls displace them in most moose populations.

Buddy never seemed to acquire the necessary skills. They spent the rut wandering from group to group, at times losing fights, but often not even bothering to challenge the bosses. Occasionally they found cows away from rutting groups and spent time with them. Often another, larger bull would arrive just as a cow was ready to mate and drive off the hapless, hopeful suitor. But Chip and Buddy reaped one benefit from their lives of few fights and rare matings: Both lived longer than average and died from causes other than fighting.

By six or seven years of age bulls like Big Boy are large enough and have enough experience to hold groups of their own, if only for a brief time until older, more experienced rivals displace them. If they are skillful and lucky, they will survive and bide their time until the following year, when perhaps a few of the older bulls will die, thereby creating openings for newcomers. This was the path that Big Boy followed.

I first saw how different Big Boy was from most other bulls on a warm September day early in the rut, when he was about eight. He had a group of about a dozen cows separated from another group of similar size a half mile away. Something spooked Big Boy's cows and they began to run toward the other group, with Big Boy bringing up the rear. By the time they reached the second group, they were overheated. Instead of immediately approaching the rival bull, Big Boy lay down and rested while the other bull gathered up all the cows for himself. After thirty minutes, a cooler, rested Big Boy confidently challenged the other bull and after a brief fight claimed all the cows as his own.

Later that year I watched as Big Boy fought another bull and lost the uphill advantage. A bull learns early in his fighting career that when you are battling sixteen hundred pounds of determined power, it pays to be on the uphill side and use gravity to your advantage. As the fight progressed

Mature bulls have the size and experience necessary to be dominant breeding bulls by the time they reach six to seven years of age.

Bulls that lose too much weight during the autumn rutting season may not survive severe winters.

and Big Boy tired, he lost his footing during a clash and went down. With aggressive opponents, this can be a fatal mistake, and I fully expected to see a serious goring. But Big Boy kept perfectly still, barely breathing. His rival stood over him for a minute or two, but soon decided Big Boy was no longer a threat and quickly walked off. Big Boy stayed down until the other bull was out of sight, then rose and calmly wandered away.

Biologists are taught that while moose and other animals are superbly adapted to their environments and learn many things that are necessary to survive, they don't make decisions. Instead, they rely greatly on instincts, patterned behaviors carried in their genes. After many years of observing moose, it appears to me that they do make important decisions every day. They must decide where to go, what to eat, how to interact with other moose, how to cope with severe weather, and a host of other issues. In life-or-death situations, I have watched them carefully assess options and make choices. Interacting often with bears and wolves that constantly try to kill them, moose must decide whether to avoid or evade, stand or run, defend or not, and then execute these strategies given many different types of terrain, vegetation, and weather conditions, all of which require different choices at different times.

Big Boy showed me that moose do make important decisions, choices that affect their well-being and survival. Had he rushed right in against a well-rested, cooler opponent and immediately initiated a fight, the risk of losing would have been too great. Somehow he knew this. Had he struggled to regain his footing while down, he would have been gored and injured. Better to remain motionless. Big Boy somehow made the right decisions. To me, they involved more than just instinct.

Areas used by bulls during winter accumulate shed antlers. Sheds persist several years before rodents consume parts of them or they decompose.

During the time that Big Boy was in his prime, as I traveled to Denali for spring fieldwork, I always wondered if I would find him in good health. Winter is the critical time for moose as they struggle against deep snow that buries food and increases the costs of movement. Having not seen him for several months, I was always a little worried that snow, cold, and hunger might have taken their toll and I would follow his radio signal to a pile of bones and hair. Or maybe the ever-present wolves caught him in deep snow in a creek bottom, perhaps weakened from hunger or rutting injuries, and he lost the battle.

But each spring my fears evaporated as I found him alive and well and starting to recuperate from winter.

One of my research colleagues spent portions of several winters at Denali trying to understand how moose cope with winter. He learned that older bulls like Big Boy segregate from younger bulls and cows and spend the winter in isolated, small valleys where their favorite foods grow lush and thick. Winter foods are typically willow shrubs that find moist conditions in the valleys ideal for growth. Certain valleys support older bulls every winter from November to April. During this time bulls shed their antlers, and these accumulate over the years in various stages of decomposition as rodents gnaw them and microorganisms soften the dense bone. The valley that Big Boy liked had many such antlers; they stood out from the air as I flew over the valley counting moose. In addition to rutting behavior, we were studying antler size, composition, and structure, and I vowed to visit this valley in spring to examine sheds and obtain data.

On a bright spring morning after snowmelt and before greenup, I walked up the narrow valley and spent a pleasant day searching for antlers near the rushing stream. In the willows, several species of songbirds were busy laying out territories and getting ready to raise their young. By midmorning I had found about a dozen sheds. Suddenly I saw a large antler at the base of a spruce tree and instantly recognized it as Big Boy's. Later examination of photographs from the previous fall proved me correct. The rodents had not found it and the snow cover prevented the sun from bleaching it, so it looked just as it did when Big Boy wore it. I found where several chips were missing from a few tines as a result of fights, and the antler still had the faint odor of the rut. I put it and several others on a pack frame and carried them back for more analysis, but the antler had more value to me than just as a scientific specimen. It was a part of Big Boy, and I treasured it.

By spring large bull moose have lost about 20 percent or more of their fall body weight from a combination of rutting and the long winter. They stop eating for two weeks during the rut. As a result, the pounds melt away and they enter the winter much thinner than cows that feed throughout the rut. As snow buries forage, moose are left with coarse, fibrous twigs that provide poor nutrition, comparable to humans trying to survive only on a diet of corn flakes. How glad moose must be to finally experience spring, to watch the snow melt, and to suddenly have green, nutritious forage in abundance and variety as new leaves sprout!

Big Boy would spend each summer in a home range of about fifteen square miles that met all his needs. He spent the vast majority of his time feeding, resting, and moving from place to place. In summer moose process enormous quantities of food, extracting energy for growth, fat storage, replacement of their coats, and the production of antlers. For a moose like Big Boy that meant growing a large set of antlers weighing perhaps 60 pounds. All of the calcium and phosphorus required would come from plants in his diet, with about half of the total antler growth achieved during the month of June. It also meant laying down about 250 or more pounds of fat from early June to late August before the first frosts spoiled the banquet.

Biologists have concluded that summer nutrition is likely more important than winter nutrition for moose, as during summer they acquire the

This bull investigates its recently shed antler in early winter.

Bulls use dense stands of shrubs in summer when nutritious food is plentiful.

energy stores needed to last the rest of the year. Thus, to be successful, bulls like Big Boy must be good feeders as well as good fighters. They cannot afford to select home ranges or feeding sites with few nutritious plants, or to waste time and energy moving a lot. Nor can they burn up valuable energy interacting much with other moose. By the start of the rut, Big Boy was always fat with large, strong antlers, due largely to the good choices he made during summer.

By mid-August when I traveled north to begin fall fieldwork each year, there was already a hint of fall color on the tundra. Some years it snowed before the leaves turned. Autumn in Denali means foggy, damp days followed by bright blue skies, sandhill crane migrations, cold nights with heavy morning frosts, brilliant red bearberry leaves, heavy blueberry and cranberry crops, and the promise of winter that could come within a month. But for me, autumn meant the moose rut was at hand.

Winter for moose mostly involves surviving, and summer is mainly for feeding, but fall is for mating. Moose are often solitary during much of the year. At times they avoid other moose or are aggressive when they do encounter them. They mainly associate with others when they happen to jointly occupy patches of good habitat. Then there is very little social behavior and no interest at all in sex. The reproductive systems of bulls are totally shut down for about eight months each year. But in late summer

Brilliant leaf colors signal the start
of the rut for moose each year.

moose begin to associate much more, hormones are turned back on, and bulls go through the human equivalent of puberty, not once in a lifetime, but annually.

The rut begins with the shedding of antler velvet, the dark skin that covers antlers during growth. Mating starts about September 25, so there is a full month of prerutting activity that involves numerous behaviors seen only at this time of year. Throughout this period bulls sort out their dominance hierarchy, and by mid-September the top bulls have collected groups of cows that will stay in the same general areas until mating is complete.

After Big Boy reached his prime, I selected him and his group as the focus of my rutting observations. He held the largest group of cows in the area, so my time there was well spent as cows came and left and a constant parade of challenger bulls passed by. Each day we arose early and took the one-hour hike to his rutting area. Some years there was a foot of snow and ten-degree temperatures during the peak of the rut; other years had shirt-sleeve weather in early October. Once there, we located the radioed animals, counted all the moose in the group and around the fringes, and spent the day recording the occurrence and frequency of all the behaviors we could see. After a time, recording numerous instances of common behaviors got tedious, but this was soon forgotten when Big Boy and one of his rivals decided to fight.

Bulls use threats and displays to establish dominance ranks.

Fights are preceded by intense displays with each bull showing his antler and body size.

Because the rutting group was often spread out over a large area, typically in dense spruce forest, and because we focused at times on behavior of radioed cows, the first hint of a fight often was the sound of a tremendous clash of antlers. My colleagues and I and perhaps a photographer or two would then run there to see the spectacle. My job was to stay close enough to record the behaviors, determine the outcome, and note things like instances of broken antlers, all without being too close to risk being run over accidentally. The moose were totally engrossed with each other and ignored their human audience.

During the three years that Big Boy was about nine to eleven years old, he was the only bull we studied that was able to hold a rutting group during the entire mating season each year. Other bulls might hold a group only a day or two before being defeated by a rival, or might hold on until intense rutting activity drained their energy or robbed their confidence. I calculated that from beginning to end, Big Boy might have fought as many as twelve battles per year, with perhaps three or four of those being epic contests that severely tested his endurance. This was a remarkable achievement, comparable to a human boxer winning several championship bouts during a two-week period without suffering major injuries.

While other bulls like Chip and Buddy might mate with only two or three cows a year, Big Boy reaped the rewards of his efficient summer feeding, his good choice of winter habitat, his superior genes, and his exceptional fighting ability by mating with up to twenty-five females each year. Over his lifetime, his success was measured by leaving behind many more descendants than lesser bulls despite the high mortality of calves. Each year since his reign, I have looked carefully at all the bulls and cows that now inhabit his old territory, wondering how many carry his genes. And I wonder if any of them, as individuals, will match his remarkable success.

When I first saw Big Boy in early September of what was to be his last year, I knew that he was declining. He wasn't as fat as in recent years, his antlers were less massive, and he was stiff, perhaps from arthritis in his hips or back. But things that year progressed right on schedule during the rut, with Big Boy gathering a large group of cows in the same area where he had held court for several years. Despite his decline, he was still the "baddest" moose in the area. Perhaps most of the other bulls didn't even try to challenge him, remembering the results of challenges in prior years. As the peak of the rut approached, I assumed that Big Boy would make it through his fourth year of being undefeated.

During the last week of September, as mating began, several of my radioed cows were part of Big Boy's large group. They chose this area each year and faithfully returned to it during the rut, as most mature cows do. Big Boy had sired their calves for three years, and I was anxious to see if this pattern would be repeated. Two radioed cows mated early with Big Boy, as did several uncollared others. Five or six lesser bulls were hanging around the edges of the group, but none was a serious challenger. Big Boy only needed to approach them, at times making half-hearted charges, for them to retreat and leave the cows alone.

As a television cameraman and I walked to the rutting grounds on a cold October morning, I thought we would find things as we left them the night before. But a new bull was in charge of the cows that morning, and

Fights end when one bull runs off while the winner tries to gore him.

Big Boy was nowhere in sight. I was so confident in Big Boy that I had left my radio receiver behind and now had to search for him by sight. When I found him nearby, he had obviously been in a fight, although he was lying down and the extent of his injuries was not apparent. Only when he tried to stand did I realize how serious it was. One or both of his rear legs were severely injured and he couldn't walk. I stayed with him for about two hours, when suddenly the new bull arrived and gored him again, on the ground. A bull like this has no defense and is at the mercy of his rival. This time, his rival was merciless.

When we left that night, Big Boy was still alive but couldn't lift his head. I knew it was the last time I would see him alive, so before we left I spent a few minutes with him thinking about all the days we spent together and how much I had learned. I told him he was a hell of a moose and wished him well in his next life.

Surely Big Boy knew he was old and not as strong as he had been. He definitely knew he could back down from his last fight; the rules of moose fighting provide room for a quick exit. Had he exited, he likely would have lived another year or two, dying at last from starvation or wolves, a fall through the ice, or perhaps a lingering infection. But Big Boy did not quit. How could he? He was a warrior to the end, and most warriors die by the sword. They really have little choice.

Certain bulls attain exceptional reproductive success by virtue of their superior genetics.

Two years after he died, on the anniversary of his death, I went back for a final visit. Daylight was fading fast and I had a long hike back to my truck, but I stayed awhile. There remained a few bleached bones along with the skull and antlers. The porcupines and hares had reduced the antlers somewhat, but their massive bulk was still apparent. A light snowfall covered them, and a red fox had left a few pawprints on one antler palm.

I'd like to think that the old skull is still there proving that Big Boy once lived, but I don't plan to go check. I don't want to risk finding nothing.

A young female moose during spring when calves are born and nutritious green leaves become available after a long winter.

The Right Stuff

In 1998 some of my radio-collared female moose died, and in August I went to Denali to look for replacements. In previous years I'd learned that if I collared moose in certain areas, they were likely to spend most of their time far from the park's road and were therefore difficult to observe. But in certain other areas, collared moose were likely to remain accessible and I could more efficiently observe them.

I chose one of my favorite places to collar moose and parked my truck next to the road. My capture gear was quickly placed in my pack—dart gun, darts, immobilizing drug, collars, and other equipment—and I entered the forest. This area of open forest was ideal for collaring moose. After the dart strikes and the moose runs off a short distance, if the cover is too dense, contact with the moose may be lost. It takes up to twenty minutes for the drug to work, so continuous observation is important.

I quickly encountered three adult female moose browsing on willows. I carefully evaluated them to see which one might be a good candidate for collaring. They were all quite tolerant of me, an important factor as I'd learned previously that intolerant moose were difficult to observe and often did not become more tolerant over time. Young females were the best candidates for collaring as I wanted animals I could observe over many years.

One female met my criteria. I loaded the dart gun, fired the dart and watched as she continued to feed before suddenly collapsing. The collar was bolted around her neck, basic information was recorded, and forty minutes later she stood and moved off. This young female was much like the scores of other females I'd collared in previous years. I had no reason to believe that she was special, but in the next fifteen years I would spend many days with her and discover how truly special she was.

A radio-collared moose named Maggie I followed for fifteen years feeds on willows in early spring.

I named this moose Maggie. She appeared to be three or four years old and in fine condition. She had no calves with her but might have lost calves earlier in the summer as did most of the cows in the area at that time. Predation, mostly by grizzly bears, was common, and some years only ten percent of the moose calves survived.

The next year I was not in the field during spring and did not know if Maggie had calves, but if she did they were gone by September when I observed her alone. That fall she wandered over a large area, at times moving far from the road and living in places I could not easily reach.

By the time Maggie was five to six years old in 2000, she was entering her peak reproductive years. That spring I found her in the park's entrance area accompanied by a set of twins. This area is highly developed, and from May to September hundreds of thousands of park visitors pass through here. The railroad runs through the area, and several freight and passenger trains pass through each day, some pausing at the train station to discharge or pick up hundreds of passengers. There is a big visitor center that attracts large numbers of people, and a science and learning center nearby. The park's post office and mercantile store are adjacent to the largest campground in the park. And, of course, each day hundreds of cars, trucks, and busses crowd the park's road that runs through the heart of the entrance area.

Despite all this development and human activity, female moose have long chosen the park's entrance area as a place to have calves. During the more than three decades that I've worked in the park, I've observed several females with calves each year in that area. I think female moose have given birth here for hundreds or thousands of years mainly because the area is low in elevation and green leaves appear here up to three weeks earlier than elsewhere. The highly nutritious leaves are critical for milk production, and females with access to them need not rely on depleting their limited energy reserves as they struggle to produce enough milk to raise calves.

But not all female moose were likely to choose the entrance area as a place to raise calves. Many females are intolerant of the extreme human presence. I think the moose that are tolerant were likely born here themselves. From their earliest days they were exposed to the human activity and learned how to survive alongside it. They then returned as adults to raise their own calves in the area and to carry on the tradition.

For the next ten years Maggie returned to the park's entrance area each spring and produced seventeen calves, including seven sets of twins. Her pattern remained the same each year. She would arrive in the area in early

May accompanied by her yearling calves. As her late May delivery date approached she would be increasingly aggressive toward her yearlings, charging them repeatedly despite their reluctance to leave. Her birth sites were in small patches of dense forest often only short distances from roads or buildings. For the next six to eight weeks as the calves grew, Maggie would remain in this area, eventually leaving to move farther west. By September she and her calves reached the far western end of her home range about fifteen miles from the entrance area. Here, she would spend the fall mating season. I was not in the field during winter so never learned where she lived, but during some years she arrived at the park's sled dog kennels in late winter, at times aggressively charging the dogs but never injuring them.

Prior to collaring Maggie I observed cows with young calves when opportunities arose, but it was often difficult to learn much, especially when females aggressively protected their calves. Many female moose are notoriously dangerous when they have young calves, but there is a lot of variation among them. Maggie proved to be extremely tolerant of people and provided me with many wonderful opportunities to learn a great deal

About one-half of all moose calf births at Denali National Park are twins like these.

Some female moose are highly tolerant of people and raise their calves in developed areas.

about the early life of calves. Many of my other collared moose gave birth in areas that were difficult to access, and observing them was inefficient as a result. But because Maggie lived in the park's entrance area and because she was radio-collared I was able to observe her and her calves every day.

During the first month of life for the calves, their daily schedule remained quite consistent. Maggie had to feed as much as possible during about seven activity bouts each day that lasted one to two hours each for a total feeding time of about ten hours per day. Activity bouts occurred uniformly during the day and night. They were separated by resting bouts of two to three hours each. Maggie's schedule was quite predictable, so I was able to observe her during an activity bout and then leave to check on my other moose before returning in time to observe the next feeding period. My days were often twelve or more hours long as I tried to observe as much as possible.

Biologists studying members of the deer family long ago observed different patterns of calves or fawns associating with their mothers. Certain species like white-tailed deer stash their fawns in safe places and infrequently tend them, while other species like moose are never far from their young. These two patterns were termed "hiders" and "followers." Prior to Maggie, I observed many cases of females feeding far from their resting calves and wondered how accurate the "follower" label was. During a five-year period I compiled a good record of Maggie's feeding bouts

Young calves like this one are born in late May.

when she had calves with her compared to when she left them behind. During 148 feeding bouts, calves were with her 52 percent of the time. They were left behind nearly half the time as Maggie fed up to a quarter of a mile away. But Maggie invariably returned to her calves at the end of activity bouts as predicted by the "follower" pattern.

Although young moose calves start feeding on plants when they are only a few days old, most of their nutrition comes from milk. Calves generally nurse at the beginning and the end of activity bouts. As soon as Maggie stood up after a two or three hour rest, the calves would quickly begin nursing while vigorously bunting Maggie's udder to stimulate milk flow. Similarly, after feeding, Maggie would stand for several minutes while the calves nursed. If there were seven feeding periods each day, the calves would nurse about fourteen times.

Biologists studying moose have estimated how much milk a female moose produces during the months that she must nurse calves. Peak production of 12.1 pounds per day occurred about one month after birth for a cow nursing a single calf. This dropped to 3.3 pounds per day when the calves were four months old and getting most of their nutrition from plants. Cows nursing two calves were estimated to produce 67 percent more milk than cows nursing only one.

Although moose produce far less milk than dairy cows, their milk is of much higher quality. It has a very strong flavor as I learned at a moose farm in Russia. During an international moose conference that included a field trip to a remote facility where female moose were kept for milk production,

Maggie's two-year-old daughter encountered a volleyball net during their travels through the park's entrance area.

Twin calves frequently nuzzle each other and play together.

I tasted moose milk. It was not an experience I would recommend to others. The Russians claim that moose milk has great healing powers for digestive system disorders. I think I'd prefer to find other remedies.

Observing Maggie's calves over the years not only allowed me to learn much about how they led their lives, but also gave me an appreciation of what wonderful little creatures they were. Their beauty was obvious. Their thick, rich, chestnut-colored coats and big eyes and ears appeal to everyone. Spindly long legs are cute despite being awkward. But their behavior interested me most, and over the course of hundreds of hours of observations I saw pretty much everything that young moose do.

Calves have strong instincts to remain close to their mothers. When Maggie and her calves were feeding near roadsides with heavy vehicle traffic nearby, I often worried that a calf would bolt out onto the road and be struck by a vehicle. Fortunately, it never happened. Even though the calves were young and inexperienced, they somehow knew that they must stay close to their mother.

Prior to Maggie, I thought that calves seldom played. I saw limited play while observing them. But I learned from watching Maggie's calves that they actually play a lot, especially when they are near water. One of Maggie's favorite places to take her calves year after year was a small pool of water at a large campground. It was located between two campsites and was surrounded by dense spruce trees. At times, Maggie and her calves would spend several days near the pool, drinking from it and laying in it on warm days. While there, the calves seldom missed an opportunity to romp through the water, running and splashing and butting heads with each other. The running would sometimes take them 50 yards or more from the

Calves nurse frequently and obtain most of their nutrition from milk during their first six weeks of life.

pool before they returned to splash again. When the calves ran off, Maggie was anxious and sometimes would run to the calves to check on their safety.

At times, calves solicited play from Maggie by approaching her with their ears lowered, a classic moose threat display, and trying to head-butt her. For the most part, Maggie ignored these overtures. During her activity bouts she was totally focused on feeding and reluctant to interact much with the calves other than to nurse them.

The park's entrance area where Maggie raised her calves contained a lot of objects that interested curious young calves, and they seldom missed an opportunity to explore them. There were orange road cones, signs of various kinds, metal gates, parked vehicles, and green electrical boxes. Whenever the calves encountered these objects they smelled them thoroughly and sometimes even tasted them. If the calves were playful, certain objects became the center of short dashes back and forth as they enjoyed the novelty of things not present in the forest.

The large campground in the entrance area provided all sorts of things of interest to the calves. There were picnic tables and fire pits that often retained food odors. There were small, orange signs that warned of bears in the area hunting moose calves and urging people to be alert. And of course, there were tents and campers to explore. These were often unoccupied during the day as people ventured out into the park. Tents seemed to be especially interesting to the calves, and they were often explored for lengthy periods.

The campground had volunteer hosts each year who typically had large campers and often had various items stored at their campsites. One year a host had several large flowerpots behind his camper, and I watched as a set of Maggie's twins encountered the pots and pulled out most of the young flowers. I'm sure the host was puzzled when he discovered the missing flowers, and he never knew that moose calves were guilty of the crime. For my part, I never confessed that I witnessed the event.

Over the years, many people were treated to the sight of Maggie and her calves as they wandered through the campground. Most of them knew to watch the moose from a safe distance. Some were able to observe nearby calves from the windows of their campers. This was a rare opportunity to be near moose calves for extended periods, and many people left the park with memories and photographs of their experiences. In other places away from the park's entrance, female moose generally were far less tolerant of people and vehicles and typically would seldom remain visible for more than a few minutes.

Maggie and her calves living in a highly developed area among thousands of park visitors and campers also created potentially serious problems. Although Maggie was extremely tolerant of people, she had limits because she was a moose with the same strong drive to protect her calves that all female moose have. It took a lot to provoke her, but when she felt her calves were threatened she responded.

I experienced her aggression firsthand. One day I observed Maggie and her calves during an early morning activity bout, and I then left to check on another moose while Maggie rested. I returned about two hours later and found the calves resting where I'd last seen them, but Maggie was feeding next to the road about two hundred yards away. I approached her carrying my radio receiver and antenna, and when I was halfway there she suddenly ran down the road toward me. I retreated, but she was gaining fast, so I darted into the woods and dropped my gear. She entered the woods, and I ran back to the roadside. Somewhere along the way I tore my hamstring, causing me to limp around for a week or two. In retrospect, I think Maggie was searching for her calves and not very interested in me, but when an animal as big as a moose appears to be charging it's easy to panic.

During hundreds of days of observations I recorded many incidents when Maggie aggressively responded to people who she felt were threatening her calves. Over a six-year period I saw 53 incidents. Most were not serious and consisted of a bluff charge where the moose ran a short distance

Young calves explore strange objects they encounter as they move through developed areas.

Cows may court bulls when they are receptive to mating.

toward someone, causing the person to retreat. But others could have resulted in serious injuries. Fortunately, Maggie always retreated and never tried to injure anyone despite ample opportunities to do so.

Many park visitors carry pepper spray to ward off bear attacks. One morning a young woman blundered onto Maggie and her calves and was charged. She tried to spray the moose but wind blew the spray back at her, and she received more of it than did the moose. The defensive use of pepper spray has its limits.

On another occasion I witnessed Maggie and her calves feeding by the side of a walking trail next to the campground. Two young girls rode their pink bicycles down the trail right up to the moose and then screamed as the moose charged. The outcome could have been bad, but once again Maggie failed to injure anyone.

While Maggie exercised restraint in dealing with people, she made up for it when dealing with dogs. To her, dogs, no matter their size, were no different than wolves, which for thousands of years have preyed on moose calves. Female moose evolved their aggressive behavior largely to defend themselves and their calves from wolf predation.

Many campers at Denali brought dogs with them, at times ignoring the requirement to keep them leashed. When unleashed dogs encountered moose in the campground, there was always the potential for injuries to

By late August, mature bulls have fully-grown antlers and are preparing to enter the rutting season when mating occurs.

dogs, calves, or people trying to save their dogs. Even when dogs were leashed, problems could occur as Maggie never realized that leashed dogs posed little danger.

A few incidents involving dogs firmly remain in my memory. One evening when Maggie and her calves were resting between two campsites, a camper pulled into an adjacent site. A man attached a long chain to the rear of the camper and clipped the other end to the collar of a large dog. Maggie approached the dog, which promptly wrapped the chain around a small spruce tree thereby preventing any escape. I think the dog survived only because the calves were far enough away, or perhaps Maggie had learned from her sled dog kennel visits that chained dogs pose little threat.

On another occasion a friend of mine pulled into the campground to dispose of some garbage. She had a large wolf-like dog on a leash as she left her vehicle. Maggie was nearby and charged. My friend panicked and could not get free of the leash as the moose kicked the dog in its back with a glancing blow. Other than being sore for a few days the dog survived. My friendship with the woman was tested after that as she persisted in saying bad things about my favorite female moose.

Then one year there was an elderly campground host with a large dog that he walked through the campground several times each day. I tried to warn him about the danger of encountering Maggie when he was out with

Bulls and cows seek each other out during the monthlong rutting season that includes mating in late September.

By September, calves have grown to about 300 pounds and have shed their chestnut-colored coats.

his dog, but evidently he was unconcerned. One day he left his camper with the leashed dog in tow only to encounter Maggie nearby. She charged, and the man fell, breaking a bone in his wrist. Fortunately, the moose contacted neither the man nor the dog.

Throughout this entire time, Park Service personnel tried to manage moose-human interactions in the entrance area in order to protect people from moose and to ensure that moose could survive. Maggie was not the only moose living in this area, but she was the one most commonly in close proximity to people. If there were incidents, a park ranger or a wildlife technician would arrive on the scene and try to keep people away from the moose. Generally everything turned out fine, and when Maggie quit feeding and began resting everyone left the area.

By late June during most years, Maggie spent less time close to people, and by mid-July when her calves were two months old, she typically left the entrance area and moved far to the west. However, one year she persisted in living in the campground and near the visitor center. There were incidents every day and Park Service personnel monitored them continuously. Finally, out of frustration, a park ranger fired rubber bullets at her to no avail. Had he asked, I would have advised that moose generally react poorly to attempts to haze them.

Two months later Maggie's radio-collar was failing, and it was time to replace it. I located her with her twin calves in a suitable location and loaded my dart gun. As I approached her she ran off, perhaps because she remembered the rubber bullet treatment and did not want to experience it

By choosing large, mature, dominant bulls as mates, cows may improve the survival of their calves.

again. After several more approaches I finally got near enough to dart her. She ran into some dense cover and disappeared. I was not concerned with losing track of her because I could easily home in on her radio, but when I turned on the receiver there was no signal. Sometimes when moose are immobilized they can end up in a bad position and have trouble breathing, so it is critical to quickly locate them. I knew my only chance of finding her was to see the calves standing nearby, so I began searching and soon located them. Maggie was breathing well, and I quickly removed her old collar and installed a new one. I was lucky to find her on that day and knew there might have been a much different outcome.

After documenting Maggie's calf production and survival during her peak reproductive years and comparing her reproductive success with my other collared females, I realized that she was far more successful than most of the others. She was pregnant every year during a ten-year period and produced seventeen calves. Of these, at least eight survived one full year and most likely survived to become adults. Many of my other collared females produced only one or two surviving calves during their lifetimes. I began to think of possible reasons why some females were much more successful at reproduction than others. Clearly, not all females were alike. Just as some males like Big Boy were exceptional, some females like Maggie contributed more of their genes to future generations than did other females.

Perhaps Maggie's success was largely due to her choice of the park's entrance area as a place to give birth year after year. Surely the early development of green leaves that had about four times as much protein as twigs allowed her to produce more milk and higher quality milk than females living at higher elevations where growth of leaves was delayed. And even though bears preyed on moose calves in the entrance area, they did so at lower rates than elsewhere, so Maggie's calves had good odds of surviving their critical first six weeks. After she left the entrance area in midsummer, Maggie still had to choose places where she could avoid and evade predators during the rest of the year. The high survival rate of her yearlings was proof that she was able to do this.

Perhaps some females have lower reproductive success because, unlike Maggie, they fail to become pregnant every year. Research has shown that well-nourished female moose during their prime reproductive years have high pregnancy rates often exceeding 90 percent. This can drop dramatically when food is inadequate. High-quality food is abundant in most places at Denali, and all the females I followed were pregnant every year until they reached old age. Reproductive success, therefore, was more a function of calf survival than of calf production.

Perhaps some female moose are better mothers than others. They might be more vigilant and able to better detect and avoid danger than other females. They might be more attentive to their calves. They might be better at finding nutritious food for their calves and themselves and might be more efficient at producing high-quality milk. These variables are all difficult to assess, but it's likely that they do play important roles in calf survival.

Differences among female moose that determine reproductive success are important, but they are only part of the story. Calves get one-half their

When she was older and failed to give birth to calves, Maggie remained bonded with her daughter for two years.

genes from their fathers. Perhaps some bulls are more fit than others and they pass this on to their offspring. If there are marked differences among bulls in their ability to produce strong, viable calves with high survival rates, perhaps females can detect differences in male fitness and choose to mate with certain bulls or certain types of bulls while rejecting others.

We learned during our rutting behavior studies at Denali that large, mature bulls do most of the mating by defending groups of females from rival bulls. Female groups form about two weeks before mating begins. Females have several options: they can remain apart from a group and mate with bulls that locate and court them, bulls that may be unable to compete well with other bulls or defend female groups of their own. Alternatively, females may join a group and remain with it or may leave and join another group. By selecting a group to join, a female cannot select a particular bull to be her mate as she cannot predict whether or not the dominant bull at the time will remain dominant when she is ready to mate or will be displaced by a rival. But she can ensure that no matter which particular bull prevails, he will have demonstrated his fitness by surviving to maturity and achieving dominance over other bulls.

And so, at conception, the earliest stage of reproduction, important behavioral choices by females may help determine their reproductive success. Their own ability to produce and rear calves combined with choices they make in selecting their mates interact to influence their reproductive success.

One of the most prominent female rutting behaviors I observed early in my Denali research was the loud, wavering, plaintive vocalization that commonly occurred in response to courtship by bulls. My colleagues and I soon realized that it was not a mating call advertising a female's receptivity, but actually was just the opposite. Females were protesting unwanted courtship, and we named the vocalizations protest moans. We began a field study to see if we could link protest moans to female mate choice, and we collected data over the next several years to test our predictions.

We thought that if protest moans reduced female harassment by bulls through fomenting combat among males, this would demonstrate subtle, indirect mate choice by females. We predicted that females should moan more frequently when courted by small bulls and less often when courted by large males. Rates of aggression among males should also be elevated following protest moans.

By examining the timing of over one thousand protest moans that we observed, we found that the frequency of moans was closely associated with mating behavior. Females decreased rates of protest moans with increasing size of males. Clearly, unwanted courtship by small males elicited strong protests from females. Females were much less likely to protest courtship by large males.

As predicted, protest moans stimulated aggression among males. Aggressive interactions were more than twice as likely to occur during

One of Maggie's seventeen calves produced during ten years when she was observed at Denali National Park.

time periods following protest moans than during periods lacking moans. By moaning loudly in response to unwanted courtship by small males, females drew the attention of large males that aggressively displaced their smaller rivals. Females incited aggressive behavior among males to gain an element of indirect mate choice. Females help set conditions for competition among males and thereby increase their likelihood of mating with a successful competitor.

In the spring of 2010 when Maggie was fifteen or sixteen years old I found her accompanied by her yearling near the sled dog kennels. She was causing some disruption so Park Service employees tried to haze her away but once again had limited success. I found her to be quite thin and bony, and she did not appear pregnant.

In time, Maggie and her yearling traveled back to the park's entrance area just as she had every year since she was young. The pair fed on new aspen leaves in open areas along the roadside and visited many of the same places used for feeding in the past. They moved into the campground for a few days, but now there were new resident moose. Several females with calves were in the area. Even though she was uncollared, I followed one female as closely as I had followed Maggie in prior years. She was young and had a single calf, perhaps her first. She was even more tolerant of people than Maggie was and stayed in the campground for a prolonged period, all the while calmly interacting with vehicles, people, and dogs. I observed many occasions where people approached the calves closely but this female did not threaten them. I have no proof, but it seems likely that this moose was one of Maggie's daughters as were some of the other females in the area. I can't imagine that moose could display this level of tolerance unless they were born and raised here and learned to be tolerant early in life.

I monitored Maggie every day to determine whether or not she had a calf. There was no evidence that she gave birth, and I saw no aggression toward her yearling, which would have been a telltale sign that birth was imminent. In fact, Maggie groomed her calf by licking her on a few occasions. It is not unusual for females of this age to skip producing new calves and to remain bonded to their yearlings for a time.

The following year I found Maggie with her two-year-old daughter in all the same places she'd been during previous years. The bond between the pair was strong, and they reminded me of Missy and Junior Miss. There was again no evidence that Maggie gave birth and no aggression toward her daughter. The campground female was back, this time with twin calves, and they used the exact same places Maggie used when she raised calves there, including the small puddle. I watched the calves romping and playing in the water, and it was very satisfying for me to think that as Maggie approached the end of her life, her unusual success at rearing calves ensured that her genes would be passed on. It occurred to me that Maggie was the female equivalent of Big Boy. Both of them had the right stuff. Maggie's exceptional ability to produce and nurture calves combined with her sound choice of mates resulted in surviving offspring that would carry on after she was gone. That was her job in life, and she did it well. It was a real pleasure to know her.